THE 7 MOST IMPORTANT

equations

FOR YOUR

retirement

Other books by Moshe A. Milevsky

Strategic Financial Planning over the Lifecycle: A Conceptual Approach to Personal Risk Management with N. Charupat and H. Huang (Cambridge, 2012)

Your Money Milestones (FT Press, 2010)

Pensionize™ Your Nest Egg with A. Macqueen (Wiley, 2010)

Are You a Stock or a Bond? (FT Press, 2009)

Lifetime Financial Advice: Human Capital, Asset Allocation and Insurance with R. Ibbotson, P. Chen and K. Zhu (CFA Institute, 2007)

The Calculus of Retirement Income (Cambridge, 2006)

Wealth Logic (Captus, 2002)

Insurance Logic with A. Gottesman (Stoddart, 2002)

Money Logic with M. Posner (Stoddart, 1999)

MOSHE A. MILEVSKY

THE 7 MOST IMPORTANT

equations

FOR YOUR

retirement

THE FASCINATING PEOPLE AND IDEAS
BEHIND PLANNING YOUR RETIREMENT INCOME

John Wiley & Sons Canada, Ltd.

Library and Archives Canada Cataloguing in Publication Data
Milevsky, Moshe Arye, 1967-
        The 7 most important equations for your retirement : the fascinating people and ideas behind planning your retirement income / Moshe A. Milevsky.

Includes bibliographical references and index.
ISBN 978-1-1182915-3-5

        1. Retirement—Planning. 2. Financial planners—Anecdotes.
I. Title. II. Title: Seven most important equations for your retirement.

HG179.M51846 2012   332.024'014   C2012-901735-3

ISBN 978-1-11834740-9 (ebk); 978-1-11834741-6 (ebk); 978-1-11834742-3 (ebk)

Production Credits
Cover design: Ian Koo
Interior text design: Laserwords
Typesetter: Laserwords
Printer: Trigraphik | LBF

John Wiley & Sons Canada, Ltd.
6045 Freemont Blvd.
Mississauga, Ontario
L5R 4J3

Printed in Canada
1 2 3 4 5 LBF TRI 16 15 14 13 12

ENVIRONMENTAL BENEFITS STATEMENT

John Wiley & Sons - Canada saved the following resources by printing the pages of this book on chlorine free paper made with 100% post-consumer waste.

TREES	WATER	ENERGY	SOLID WASTE	GREENHOUSE GASES
27	26,060	42	3,294	8,563
FULLY GROWN	GALLONS	MILLION BTUs	POUNDS	POUNDS

Environmental impact estimates were made using the Environmental Paper Network Paper Calculator. For more information visit www.papercalculator.org.

To the memory of my grandfather,
Rav Hillel Mannes, PhDc;
a German gentleman, scholar and orthodox Jew.

CONTENTS

CONTENTS

INTRODUCTION

AN EQUATION CAN'T PREDICT YOUR FUTURE ... BUT IT CAN HELP YOU PLAN FOR IT

Most books about retirement planning are written as guides, instruction manuals or "how-to" books. The authors tell you what to do, when to do it, and what to expect. I know this quite well because I have authored many such tomes myself. *Rest assured, this is not one of those books.*

This book tells stories which I hope will lead into conversations. It is a narrative involving seven people, their discoveries and the conceptual innovations that made it possible for you to stop working and enjoy the money you have accumulated, one day. These protagonists—or scientific heroes—didn't achieve their breakthroughs while hunched over a laboratory workbench, peering through a microscope or trekking through jungles. They made their discoveries sitting in front of a blank sheet of paper, but while thinking very carefully about life and money. And, like the greatest thinker of them all, Albert Einstein, they too expressed their discoveries using a very beautiful language called mathematics. Alas, the seven equations profiled in this book aren't as famous or as elegant as the simplicity of $E = MC^2$, but they are far more practical for your retirement.

You see, time is running out. North American baby boomers are getting within shouting distance of their golden years. Most have finally grasped that—despite the dreamy commercials and brochures—retirement isn't a long vacation that begins at the mythical age of 65. It's a gradual winding-down process, possibly involuntary, with austere financial implications. The timeworn questions about proper savings rates, the best mutual funds or the ideal size of your nest egg number have been pushed aside by a pragmatic economic reality: "This is what I have, give or take a few more years of saving. How do I make it last?"

In other words, it is time to have some conversations about *retirement income planning*, also known as de-accumulation planning. The stories in this book should lead you into those conversations. These conversations should take place with your family and loved ones and possibly with a professional financial advisor as well (whether you love them or not).

Reality Check

Today, there are two cold, hard facts about aging consumers heading into the second decade of the 21st century: i) most are not saving enough money to maintain their current standard of living, and ii) many are financially illiterate. Alas, study after published study continues to document a shocking lack of knowledge about basic financial affairs and a correspondingly miniscule financial cushion for retirement.

These two problems are obviously linked.

Yes, I know from many years of teaching experience that financial conversations are often dry and humorless. So I promise to do my best to lighten up the topic by keeping the technicalities to a minimum and focusing on the art.

"Art," you say?

Yes. In my mind, famous equations are like beautiful Picassos. Even if I don't quite understand the painting or the mathematics I can certainly appreciate the beauty and genius behind it. The seven equations presented in this book typify, at least for me, the conciseness, elegance and beauty that the best of the best equations demonstrate. By the end of this book, if you're not already inclined to appreciate mathematical equations for what they are, I hope you'll agree about the beauty.

Here's a brief outline of what's ahead.

In the first chapter, I will start by asking a simple question: How long will your nest egg last, if you were to stop contributing today, and instead withdraw a *fixed* amount each year while earning a *fixed* interest rate each year for the rest of your life? Although neither of these fixes are realistic in practice, this sort of analysis provides a quick and sobering assessment of whether you can maintain your standard of living, or when the money will run out if you can't. The underlying mathematics of this first equation is rather simple, and does not require any complex algorithms. Along the way, you'll learn about the 13th-century Italian educator and mathematician Leonardo Fibonacci and his remarkable technique for solving such financial problems.

In the second chapter, I'll address the length of life itself. Here is the motivating question: Given your family history, current lifestyle and recent medical experience, what are the chances that you, your spouse, or both of you, will reach age 90, 95 or even 100? In this chapter you'll learn about longevity risk and learn about the work of famous British actuary Benjamin Gompertz. He discovered and formulated the first natural law of human mortality almost 200 years ago. His equation is used daily by medical researchers, demographers and insurance specialists.

The third chapter focuses on life annuities and pensions. This is the opportunity to inquire: Do you have a true pension? I'll encourage you to dig deep into the mechanics of your employer or government retirement plan. Many are called pensions, but are basically pooled savings plans. You can however use your retirement money to buy a private pension annuity, but it can be surprisingly expensive and there are economic tradeoffs to consider. You'll also learn about the famous 17th-century astronomer and Savilian Professor of Geometry at Oxford University, Edmond Halley, who developed the first mathematical expression for the price of a life annuity. Although his full-time job was mapping the solar system and searching for comets, it seems he also had a soft spot for pensions and annuities.

In Chapter Four, I'll invite you to ponder patience. How important is it for you to enjoy your retirement money earlier rather than later? The financial industry talks about replacing 70% to 80% of your income in retirement and spending no more than 4% of your nest egg each year of retirement. But where does that number come from? Do you really want the exact *same* standard of living, regardless of how long you live? Or, are you willing to scale back if in fact you live to a ripe old age? This is yet another tradeoff, and related to the concept called *subjective time preference*. In this chapter, I argue one size doesn't fit all. I'll introduce you to the celebrated 1920s American economist and pulpit professor Irving Fisher. He formulated the precursor to financial lifecycle models and cautioned against the ravages of inflation, yet another important concern for retirees.

In Chapter Five, I address financial risk head-on. How comfortable are you with the stock market? The last quarter century has taught us that time doesn't necessarily diversify away risk. Stocks—which fluctuated more than bonds—earned less than bonds since the late 1980s. Whether this trend will persist going forward is debatable. But if stocks do continue their lackluster performance—and the economy sputters—will this impact the remaining working years of your job? In the language of financial economics, are your human capital and financial capital intertwined? If so, you might want to lay off the stocks as you get closer to retirement. Asset allocation should involve your entire personal balance sheet. In this chapter you will learn about Professor Paul Samuelson, the first American to win the Nobel Prize in Economics in 1970. He introduced an asset allocation equation that's relevant over the entire lifecycle, but especially during retirement. He was also a fierce opponent of something called *time diversification* and anyone who dared support it.

In Chapter Six, I focus your attention beyond retirement to the next generation. What do you plan to leave the kids? Is legacy a priority for you? Many who are *close to* or *in* retirement often dedicate a particular account, asset or sum for their loved ones. It's not uncommon to hear that the house is going to the kids, or that the investments will eventually go to the grandkids. This is commendable, but is it financially affordable? Here is yet another tradeoff. In fact, if legacy is your motive then you might want to see what life insurance can do for you. And vice versa: if you already have life insurance (paid up, or not) but need the money earlier, you might want to think about giving it up.

INTRODUCTION

Legacy and life insurance are important conversations to have, and this chapter is the opportunity to have those discussions. The founding father of the economics of life insurance was the charismatic teacher Dr. Solomon Huebner ("Sunny Sol" to his students) and this chapter will tell his story. You will learn about the most important equation in the life insurance business, which is naturally quite important for retirement income planning as well.

The final chapter, Chapter Seven, will pull all these strands together. I will present the one final unified equation that measures the sustainability of your retirement plan. It takes into account your age, current asset allocation, pension income, longevity and everything else on your personal balance sheet. It's a one-number summary, and the person responsible for this final equation is a Russian mathematical prodigy named Andrei Nikolaevich Kolmogorov. His life story takes us up the Volga and into the venomous politics of Stalin and the Russian Academy of Sciences.

Although the formal concept of retirement is a relatively modern phenomenon—dating to German Chancellor Otto von Bismarck's creation of the state pension, and American President Franklin D. Roosevelt's Social Security—the mathematical and statistical science behind retirement income planning is centuries old.

Looking into the future, I don't know if governments, corporations and individuals can afford to continue paying for society's current retirement promises. But one thing is certain: these seven equations and the science behind them will play a central role in the years beyond three score and 10, for many centuries to come. I hope you enjoy the mathematical, financial and historical expedition that lies ahead. I know I did.

CHAPTER 1

HOW LONG WILL MY NUMBER LAST?

EQUATION #1: LEONARDO FIBONACCI (1170–1250)

$$t = \frac{1}{r} \ln \left[\frac{c}{c - Wr} \right]$$

L eonardo had a problem. A close friend had invested some money a few years earlier in a local Italian bank, in Pisa, that promised him steady interest of 4% per month. (Yes, I wish I got 4% interest per month. I don't even get that *per year* nowadays. Sounds shady to me.) Anyway, rather than sitting by and letting the money rapidly grow and compound over time, Lenny's friend started withdrawing large and irregular sums of money from the account every few months. These sums were soon exceeding the interest he was earning and the whole process was eating heavily into his capital. To make a long story short, Leonardo—known to be quite good with numbers—was approached by this friend and asked how long the money would last if he kept up these withdrawals. Reasonable question, no?

Now, if Leonardo had been me, he'd have pulled out his handy Hewlett-Packard (HP) business calculator, entered the cash flows, pushed the relevant buttons and quickly had the answer. In fact, with any calculator these sorts of questions can be answered quite easily using the technique known as *present value analysis*—something all finance professors teach their students on the first day of class. Later, I'll explain this important process in some detail.

Unfortunately, Leonardo didn't have access to an HP business calculator that performed the necessary compound interest calculations. (He didn't have a calculator at all because they hadn't been invented yet.) You see, Leonardo was asked this question *more than 800 years ago*, in the early part of the 13th century. But to answer the question—which he certainly did—he actually invented a technique we know today as present value analysis. Yes, the one I mentioned we teach our students.

You might have heard of Leonardo by his more formal name: Leonardo Pisano *filius* ("family" in Latin) Bonacci, a.k.a. Fibonacci to the rest of the world, and probably the most famous mathematician of the Middle Ages.

In fact, Fibonacci helped solve his friend's problem—writing the first commercial mathematics textbook in recorded history in the process—and introduced a revolutionary methodology for solving complicated questions involving interest rates. Let me repeat: his technique, with only slight refinements, is still used and taught to college and university students 800 years later. Now *that* is academic immortality! (He published and his name hasn't perished yet.)

Everyone owes a debt of gratitude to Fibonacci. Had it not been for him, we would probably still be using Roman numerals in our day-to-day calculations. He helped introduce and popularize the usage of the Hindu–Arabic number system—the 10 digits from zero to nine—in the Western world by illustrating how much easier they were for doing commercial mathematics. Imagine calculating square roots or performing long division with Roman numerals. (Okay: What is XMLXVI times XVI?) Well, you can thank Leonardo.

Leonardo Fibonacci was the first financial engineer, or "quant" (translation: highly compensated, scary-smart guys and gals who use advanced mathematics to analyze financial markets) and he didn't work on Wall Street or Bay Street. He worked in the city of Pisa. More on his well-known work, and lesser-known life, later.

The Spending Rate: A Burning Question

Let's translate Fibonacci's mostly hypothetical 800-year-old puzzles into a problem with more recent implications. Imagine you're thinking about retiring and have managed to save $300,000 in your retirement account. For now, I'll stay away from discussing taxes and the exact administrative classification of the account. (I'll revisit this case in Chapter Seven, where I'll add more realistic details.) Allow me to further assume you're entitled to a retirement pension income of $25,000 per year. This is the sum total of your (government) Social Security plus other (corporate) pension plans—but the $25,000 is not enough. You need at least $55,000 per year to maintain your current standard of living. This leaves a gap of $30,000 per year, which you hope to fill with your $300,000 nest egg. The pertinent question, then, becomes: Is the $300,000 enough to fill the budget deficit of $30,000 per year? If not, how long will the money last?

As you probably suspected, your $300,000 nest egg is likely not enough. Think about it this way: the ratio of $30,000 per year (the income you want to generate) divided by the original $300,000 (your nest egg) is 10%. There is no financial instrument I'm aware of—and I've spent the last 20 years of my life searching for one—that can generate a consistent, guaranteed and reliable 10% per year. If you don't want to risk any of your hard-earned nest egg in today's volatile economic environment, the best you can hope for is about 3% after inflation is accounted for, and even that is pushing it. Sure, you might think you're earning 5% guaranteed by a bank, or 5% in dividends or 5% in bond coupons, but an inflation rate of 2% will erode the true return to a mere 3%. Needless to say, 3% will only generate $9,000 per year in interest from your $300,000 nest egg. That is a far cry from (actually $21,000 short of) the extra $30,000 you wanted to extract from the nest egg.

You have no choice. In retirement you will have to eat into your principal.

Here's a side note. In my personal experience talking to retirees and soon-to-be retirees, I find this realization is one of the most difficult concepts they must accept. Some people simply refuse to spend principal and instead submit to a reduced standard of living. Principal is sacred and they agree to live on and adapt to interest income. But in today's low-interest-rate environment, once you account for income taxes, living on interest only will eventually lead to a greatly reduced standard of living over time.

Once you accept that actually depleting your nest egg is necessary, the next—and much more relevant—question becomes: If I start depleting capital, how long before there is nothing left? After all, if you eat into the $300,000 there's a chance it might be gone, especially if you live a long time. This is exactly where Leonardo Fibonacci's insight and technique come in handy, and why I've bequeathed to him Equation #1.

Time to roll up the sleeves and get to work. Let's plug some numbers into Equation #1 and see what Fibonacci has to say.

(You might want to quickly flip back to the equation at the start of the chapter.)

Notice the right-hand side lists three variables (or inputs) that can affect the outcome. The first is the letter W, which represents the size of your nest egg, $300,000. The second variable is c, which captures the amount you would like to spend or consume, *above and beyond* any retirement pension you might be receiving. (This was $30,000 in the earlier example.) Although your spending takes place continuously (daily, weekly) it adds up to the value of c, per year. Think of it as a rate. The final variable, r, the trickiest to estimate, is the interest rate your nest egg is earning while it's being depleted, expressed in inflation-adjusted terms. That was the 3% number I mentioned earlier. Now all that's left is to compute the *natural* logarithm of the ratio, denoted by $ln[]$ in the first equation.

Natural logarithms are close cousins of common logarithms. Both buttons appear on any good business calculator, but the latter uses a base of 10 and the former a base of 2.7183. If you're unfamiliar with *natural* logarithms—or it has been a while since high-school mathematics—you can find a crash course on natural logs and how they differ from common logs in the appendix to this book.

For now, you can think (very crudely) of the natural logarithm as a process that *shrinks* numbers down to a compact size that is much easier to work with. Later you can worry about how exactly this shrinking works.

Back to the first equation. The mathematics proceeds as follows. The ratio inside the square brackets is 1.42857 written to five digits. In words, it's the desired annual consumption rate of $30,000 (above and beyond the pension income you are receiving) divided by the same consumption rate, *minus* the nest egg value ($300,000), times the investment rate (3%). Sounds wordy? I agree. That's why I—and most financial quants—prefer equations to words. But we're not done yet. Looking back at the right-hand side of the equation, now take the natural logarithm of 1.42857, which leads to 0.35667 written to five digits. Finally, and for the last step, divide this number by 0.03, which is the interest rate, and *voilà*, $t = 11.9$ years.

In words, here is the harsh truth. Keep up this lifestyle, and you'll be broke by the beginning of the 12th year of retirement spending. Not a good outcome, although you will still get your $25,000 pension for the rest of your life, which may (or may not) be enough. But the nest egg is blown. Don't feign surprise. You knew that a yearly $30,000 withdrawal (i.e., spending from the nest egg) would be too much if all you're earning is 3%. But what if you lower the withdrawal rate? Again, Fibonacci's equation, Equation #1, divulges exactly how many years of income you'll gain if you cut down on your planned spending.

Let's do this with revised values. Assume you're consuming (above the pension income you are receiving) $25,000 per year (instead of $30,000 per year), and earning the same 3% per year interest rate. In this case the item in the square brackets is 1.5625; its natural logarithm is 0.44629. When you divide by 0.03 you arrive at $t = 14.9$ years, a gain of almost three years. Here it is in words. Cut down on your planned spending by $5,000 per year and the money will last three years longer.

This standard of living is still not sustainable because there's a very good chance you'll be living in retirement more than 15 years. Okay, what if you reduce your annual (additional) withdrawals from the nest egg to $20,000? In this case the numbers are 1.81818 in the square brackets, then 0.59784 after you take natural logs and finally $t = 19.9$ years, eight years better than the original.

Is *this* good enough? Is it *long* enough? Well, that's for you to decide. Hopefully you get the point of how to "use" the equation and can generate your own values for how long the money will last. In fact, you might want to try changing the interest rate, r, which I took to be 3%. For example, if you believe (I don't) you can earn a guaranteed, safe 4% real interest rate per year, Equation #1 will result in the value of $t = 22.9$ years, if you withdraw $c = $20,000 per year and start with a $W = $300,000 nest egg. In contrast, if all you can earn guaranteed is $r = 1.5\%$ per year, your money will last $t = 17$ years. Personally, I'd lean toward using even lower values in this equation.

The input choices are infinite (no pun intended), so to help you get a better sense of the resulting values I've attached two tables with a range of output numbers. Table 1.1 assumes an investment return of 1.5%, adjusted for inflation, while Table 1.2 assumes a higher (3%) investment return, also adjusted for inflation. Again, you might think these are rather small numbers but remember these numbers are net of inflation, or what I call "real rates." If your bank is paying you 3% on your savings account, but inflation erodes 2% per year, then all you're really earning is (approximately) 1%.

Some might argue this "equation"—nominal interest earned, minus inflation rate, equals real interest—is more important than all seven equations mentioned in this entire book! If you're wondering, the person responsible for this insight is Irving Fisher, the early

Table 1.1 In How Many Years Will the Money Run Out If You Are Earning 1.5% Interest?

Nest Egg ($) →	100,000	200,000	300,000	400,000	500,000
Real Spending Rate ($)					
10,000	10.8	23.8	39.9	61.1	92.4
15,000	7.0	14.9	23.8	34.1	46.2
20,000	5.2	10.8	17.0	23.8	31.3
25,000	4.1	8.5	13.2	18.3	23.8
30,000	3.4	7.0	10.8	14.9	19.2
35,000	2.9	6.0	9.2	12.5	16.1
40,000	2.5	5.2	8.0	10.8	13.8
45,000	2.3	4.6	7.0	9.5	12.2
50,000	2.0	4.1	6.3	8.5	10.8

20th-century American economist and champion of Equation #4. No rush. We'll get to his story.

Back to the tables. The columns represent the size of your nest egg (W), and the rows represent the annual spending rate (consumption above any pension income)—also adjusted for inflation. Think of them as today's dollars.

Looking at Table 1.1, if you start retirement with $300,000 in a bank account earning 1.5% interest *every* year and you plan to withdraw $35,000 *every* year, then according to Equation #1 the money will run out in exactly 9.2 years. This is 110 months of income. That's it!

In contrast, if you reduce your spending withdrawals to $20,000 and start with the same $300,000 nest egg, your money will last 17 years. Sounds like a lot of time, but note if you retire at 65 this strategy will last (only) until you're 82.

As you'll see later in Chapter Two, when we explore patterns of longevity and mortality in retirement, there are better-than-even odds you'll still be alive at age 82. So even $20,000 from a nest egg of $300,000 (a 6.66% initial spending rate) is too high, unless you're willing to (only) live on the pension income of $25,000 once the money runs out of the nest egg. You might be willing to take that chance and trade off more money earlier in retirement in exchange for a reduced standard of living later in retirement—when you're less likely to be alive—but again, that's your choice to make after you know the numbers and odds. We will return to this economic tradeoff in Irving Fisher's Chapter Four.

Now, let's say you have $1 million in your bank account (earning 1.5%) and you plan to withdraw $50,000 per year. How long will the money last? Those values aren't directly in the table. What do you do? Well, in this case you should be able to use the equation directly (which is actually the point of this book).

Alternatively, you'll notice this equation *scales* in W and c. In other words, you can divide both W and c numbers by any number and the results don't change. So whether you have $1 million and are withdrawing $50,000, or you have $500,000 and are withdrawing $25,000, or you have $2 million and are withdrawing $100,000, they're the equivalent mathematical problem. (Although, personally, I'd obviously like to have the $2 million.) In all cases, the ratio of withdrawal-to-wealth is 1/20. Look carefully at Equation #1: only the ratio matters. On a side note, mathematicians love equations that scale. It helps do something called "reduce the dimensionality" of a problem, and eliminates the need for unnecessary information, so they tend to get excited about these things. Yes, geeky, I know.

Either way, Table 1.1 tells us that in this particular case, the money will last 23.8 years, assuming an interest rate of 1.5%.

Here's another set of values. Table 1.2 displays the left-hand side of Equation #1, but under the assumption (or input) that the interest rate on your money is $r = 3\%$ every single year, as opposed to the $r = 1.5\%$ used in Table #1. Notice that the numbers in Table 1.2 are uniformly (always) larger than the numbers in Table 1.1, and the money runs

Table 1.2 In How Many Years will the Money Run Out If You Are Earning 3% Interest?

Nest Egg ($) →	100,000	200,000	300,000	400,000	500,000
Real Spending Rate ($)					
10,000	11.9	30.5	76.8	∞	∞
15,000	7.4	17.0	30.5	53.6	∞
20,000	5.4	11.9	19.9	30.5	46.2
25,000	4.3	9.1	14.9	21.8	30.5
30,000	3.5	7.4	11.9	17.0	23.1
35,000	3.0	6.3	9.9	14.0	18.7
40,000	2.6	5.4	8.5	11.9	15.7
45,000	2.3	4.8	7.4	10.3	13.5
50,000	2.1	4.3	6.6	9.1	11.9

out later because the interest rate is 3% versus 1.5%. Hopefully the impact of increasing the projected interest rate makes intuitive sense.

As I encouraged earlier—and like all the other equations displayed in this book—you are now free to plug in your own withdrawal assumptions and interest rates.

The one thing you might wonder about is the odd-looking symbols in the upper right-hand corner of Table 1.2. They're not stray symbols or typos, but actually represent the mathematical symbol for infinity. Don't be scared. That is good news. Under these conditions the nest egg money will never run out.

Here's an explanation for why the answer is defined to be infinity, in some cases. Skip ahead if you want. Look carefully at the three cells in which the infinity symbols appear and their corresponding row and column coordinates. In particular, when your nest egg is $500,000 the 3% interest rate will generate $15,000 in annual interest. This exceeds the $10,000 you would like to extract every year. So instead of the nest egg shrinking over time, it will continue to grow! Ergo, the money will never run out. In fact, if you withdraw or consume $15,000 from the account per year, exactly the interest you are earning, the account will continue at the same $500,000 value forever. The same concept applies to the $400,000 case, where the 3% interest will generate $12,000—more than the $10,000. In all these cases the denominator within the logarithm will either be zero or negative. The logarithm of infinity (if you divide something by zero) is infinity, and the logarithm of a negative number is simply undefined. So before you use the formula on your calculator, make sure you are spending (withdrawing) more money than the interest you are earning. Otherwise, Fibonacci's equation might lead to gibberish.

Here's the bottom line with infinites. May we all be lucky enough to have large enough nest eggs relative to our withdrawal rate that Fibonacci's equation results in infinity. Most of us, unfortunately, will retire to a reality reflected in the lower left-hand corner of these tables.

Fibonacci's Fabulous Flash of Finance

The name Fibonacci is widely recognized among the bookish masses for something known as the Fibonacci series (or Fibonacci numbers), which has nothing to do with retirement finance or stock trading and more to do with sexually active rabbits. More on this later, but first let me describe Fibonacci's contributions to commercial mathematics.

To begin with, Leonardo Pisano—a.k.a. Fibonacci—wrote a very famous book called *Liber Abaci* (Latin for "Book of Calculations") whose first edition appeared around the year 1202. He revised the book a number of times (that is, he rewrote it) over the next 30 years, and only a few of these revisions are available today. The book itself was written in Latin (which I don't speak or understand). But in the year 2003—exactly eight centuries after the first edition was written—*Liber Abaci* was translated by Professor Laurence Sigler into English, a language I do speak.

To be clear, *Liber Abaci* is a textbook and probably the first text-book of its kind. It has many chapters, diagrams, theorems, proofs and many, many problems—you could think of them as homework assignments—which Fibonacci solved in painstaking detail. It is these problems and their solution methodology that are the main gems of the book. I posed one of those problems at the beginning of this chapter.

To understand the context of Fibonacci's contribution to commercial mathematics, consider the era in which he lived. In the 13th century, the city of Pisa—and most of what is today northern Italy—was at the commercial center of the world. Think of Hong Kong, London and New York squeezed into a few hundred miles. The region had 28 different vibrant cities, each issuing their own currency for trading purposes. This lively economic environment was ideal for the sorts of commercial problems Fibonacci posed and solved in *Liber Abaci*. He didn't have to make up the stories. He lived them.

Here is one of the many problems that Fibonacci posed, which may seem like just another problem but is actually the intellectual inspiration for Equation #1 in this book.

On Problems of Travellers and Also Similar Problems: A Certain man proceeding to Lucca on business to make a profit doubled his money, and he spent there 12 denari. He then left and went through Florence; he there doubled his money and he spent 12 denari. Then, he returned to Pisa; doubled his money and spent 12 denari, and it is proposed that he had nothing left. It is sought how much he had in the beginning. . . . (Sigler translation, chapter 12, page 372)

HOW LONG WILL MY NUMBER LAST?

With a little bit of imagination you can translate Fibonacci's 800-year-old traveler into a modern-day retiree who starts retirement with an unknown sum of money. That's the variable to be solved. The money is invested in a bank account that doubles its value every dozen years, an interest rate of approximately 6% per year. Now, at the end of each year, the retiree withdraws one denari (or dollar, euro, peso) from the bank account, and spends it. This growth and spending process continues for three dozen years (i.e., 36 withdrawals), at which point the money runs out. Fibonacci's question is: How much money did the retiree—who probably wants to spend his time traveling—begin with? Remember, this problem was posed 800 years ago, in the year 1200. Retirement challenges might not be as contemporary as you think.

Fibonacci formulated this problem algebraically, but his genius was in going one step further than the man who invented algebra itself, the Persian scholar Muhammed Al-Kwarizimi in 820 AD.

In Fibonacci's words, here's how he did it:

Because it is proposed that he always doubled his money, it is clear that 2 will be made from one. Whence it is seen what fraction 1 is of 2, namely ½, which thus is written three times because of the three trips that he made: ½ ½ ½, and the 2 is multiplied by the 2 and the other twos that are under the fraction; there will be 8 of which you take ½ namely 4, of which you take ½ namely 2, and of the two you take ½, namely 1. After this you add the 4 to the 2 and the 1, there will be 7 that you multiply by the 12 denari, which he spent; there will be 84 that you divide by the 8. The quotient will be **ten and one half denari**, and the man had this money. . . . (Sigler translation, chapter 12, page 373)

Did you catch it? Did you see the flash of genius? On the third line, Fibonacci invented interest discounting. Granted, he didn't have the greatest talent for explaining his inventions. Truthfully, the prose sounds more biblical rebuke than textbook pedagogy, but most scholars agree that multiplying the third cash flow by the triple fraction ½ ½ ½ and the second cash flow by ½ ½ and the first cash flow by ½, he gets the credit for introducing the world to the present value factor.

He allowed money to travel from the future into the present and back again. In fact, to ensure everyone understood his clever technique, the next 15 pages of *Liber Abaci* introduce ever more complicated traveler problems with cash flows and interest rates of different sizes using something he called the "method of trips." It seems he recognized the centrality of this technique to commercial transactions, and—as many students would demand from their modern-day instructor—solved many similar problems so it was clear to all his readers.

In sum, Fibonacci's genius was that he broke down complicated compound interest calculations—taking place across different periods of time—by bringing cash flows back to the present and manipulating those values while eliminating the messy time dimension.

So, for example, when you are told that a dollar today is worth more than a dollar next year, that is a present value statement. Or, when a bond that pays $100,000 at the end of the year is currently trading for only $96,000, the reason is present value.

In fact, in the latter part of *Liber Abaci*, Fibonacci used this technique to quantify the impact of compounding periods—annual versus quarterly, for example—involving various debt instruments and even pensions. Indeed, 800 years later, problems such as *On a Soldier Receiving Three Hundred Bezants for His Fief* (page 392), *On a Ton of Pisan Cheese* (page 137) and *On Two Men Who Had a Company in Constantinople* (page 393) could all serve as excellent homework assignments and exam questions on financial mathematics. As Professor William Goetzmann from Yale—who has done much to alert scholars to Fibonacci's contribution to finance—wrote in a survey article, "He was not only a brilliant analyst of the business problems of his day, but also a very early financial engineer whose work played a major role in Europe's distinctive capital market development in the late Middle Ages and the Renaissance."

Back to the motivating question of this chapter: How long will the money last? Fibonacci's answer is as follows.

The present value of your retirement withdrawals, from the date of retirement until the date the bank account is exhausted, must exactly equal the sum of money you started out with. This is the equation to be solved. Locating the time at which the money runs out boils down to locating a present value—as a function of time—that is equal to the initial nest egg.

Manipulating the First Equation

Equations have no feelings, so they can be manipulated and even abused without guilt or concern—as long as the rules of mathematics are obeyed. You might remember these operations from high-school algebra (or perhaps *you* felt abused by that experience). Either way, Equation #1 is ripe for manipulation. In particular you can *invert and solve* for the real interest rate (*r*) you must earn during retirement so your initial retirement nest egg (*W*) lasts for a desired number of years (*t*), assuming you're planning to spend or withdraw (*c*) per year. Likewise, you can *invert and solve* for the nest egg (*W*) required so you can spend (*c*) for exactly (*t*) years. Remember, Equation #1 involves four variables so you can place any three of them on one side to solve for the fourth.

Table 1.3 How Much Money Do You Need for a 30-Year Retirement?

Real Interest Rate (%)	Real Spending per Year			
	$25,000	$50,000	$75,000	$100,000
0.5	$ 696,460	$ 1,392,920	$ 2,089,380	$ 2,785,840
1.0	$ 647,954	$ 1,295,909	$ 1,943,863	$ 2,591,818
1.5	$ 603,953	$ 1,207,906	$ 1,811,859	$ 2,415,812
2.0	$ 563,985	$ 1,127,971	$ 1,691,956	$ 2,255,942
2.5	$ 527,633	$ 1,055,267	$ 1,582,900	$ 2,110,534
3.0	$ 494,525	$ 989,051	$ 1,483,576	$ 1,978,101
3.5	$ 464,330	$ 928,660	$ 1,392,991	$ 1,857,321
4.0	$ 436,754	$ 873,507	$ 1,310,261	$ 1,747,014
4.5	$ 411,533	$ 823,066	$ 1,234,600	$ 1,646,133
5.0	$ 388,435	$ 776,870	$ 1,165,305	$ 1,553,740

If this sounds awfully abstract, here's a very specific and practical example of why manipulation pays off. How much money must you have saved up at retirement, if you want your money to last for exactly 30 years? Think of this as your retirement goal, or "the number," as Lee Eisenberg popularized it in his bestselling book (also called *The Number*). Fibonacci's equation gives us the answer. In this case, we are trying to solve for (W) in Equation #1, by isolating it from the other variables. (I'll spare you the algebraic details, but it's actually trivial. Ask your 15-year-old.) Table 1.3 provides a number of these results.

For example, in the first row and first column of Table 1.3, at the crossroads of 0.50% interest and $25,000 withdrawing/spending, you'll see the number $696,460. This means that if all you plan on spending each year—for the planned 30 years of retirement—is $25,000 and the money (while it is waiting to be spent) is earning 0.50% (yes, that is a small number, but have you checked your bank account lately?), then you need a nest egg of $696,460 at retirement. In contrast, if you go down one row and manage to earn 1% interest per year, you don't need as much to finance the $25,000 spending.

In that case, $647,954 is enough. The extra half-percent interest rate will save you almost $48,500.

All this information can be extracted from this chapter's champion, Equation #1. But hey, don't trust me. If you plug in (insert, substitute) the value of c = $25,000 and r = 1% and W = $647,954 into the right-hand side of the equation, out pops t = 30 years on the left-hand side. Confirmed!

Is It Really His?

Although I have given credit (and ownership) of this chapter's equation, Equation #1, to Fibonacci, I must be absolutely clear: he did *not* write down the equation as it's listed in the opening title to this chapter. In fact, were he alive today he would be hard-pressed to recognize the equation largely because logarithms—which are part of the equation—weren't actually invented for another 400 years (by John Napier) and natural logarithms didn't appear until a full century after that (with credit to Leonard Euler).

Fibonacci didn't write down any equations (as we use the term today) in *Liber Abaci,* and he certainly didn't manipulate equations or solve for variables using the notation taught in today's high schools or universities.

The reason I've given him credit for this equation—written using modern day notation—is that this equation would be meaningless without the underlying concept of present value, precisely what Fibonacci deserves credit for inventing. So if he were alive today and asked me about Equation #1, it would probably take me a few minutes to explain my notation—and perhaps an hour more to explain natural logarithms. But I'm certain once I explained to him that the present value of your retirement income until the date your money runs out must equal your nest egg, he would say, "Hey, that was my idea about the trips and the denari." And he would be perfectly correct in claiming ownership; hence, he is the champion of this chapter.

Can We Really Know Interest Rates?

Now, the one thing that might bother users of this equation is the interest or investment rate. How in the world are you to figure out what your money will actually earn for the next few decades, be it in a bank account, mutual fund or anywhere else? Sure, today you might be getting 1.5%, but perhaps that will decline even more over time. What if the money is invested in the stock market, in which case r is truly random? How do you use the equation then?

Well, at the risk of getting ahead of ourselves, let me assure you that the seventh and final equation in this book—credited to the Russian mathematician Andrei Kolmogorov—is an extension of Equation #1. With that final equation we will enter a world in which you don't know exactly what your money will earn going forward, and you don't know how long you're going to live. It will bring together all the chapters and equations in this book—but I am getting way ahead of myself.

Back to Fibonacci's Life Story

Very little is known about the life of Leonardo Fibonacci. The few facts that historians have gleaned about him come from a very short one-page biography he wrote about himself in the introduction to *Liber Abaci*, as well as some official documents from the city of Pisa.

His father was a customs official posted in Bugia, a sister city and trading post of Pisa on the Barbary coast of Africa, in today's Algeria. As a young child, Fibonacci was brought by his father from

Pisa (where he was likely born in 1170) to Bugia, where he had the opportunity, as an adult, to interact with merchants from Egypt, Syria and Greece. It is likely he traveled extensively in North Africa and had the opportunity to meet with other Middle Eastern scholars of the time, where he learned the Hindu–Arabic number system and perhaps Arabic itself. Fibonacci left Bugia in his early thirties, spending his later life in Pisa—a city which has now claimed him as its own, with the requisite Italian statue in a downtown piazza. Rightfully so, since Fibonacci is one of the two great scientific luminaries from Pisa (the other being Galileo Galilei, born 200 years later).

Recall that Fibonacci was located in the banking epicenter of the world. Figure 1.1 gives an indication of how rich and complex financial life was in 13th and 14th-century Italy. Each city had its own currency and interest rate. No surprise, then, that Leonardo Fibonacci would be thinking of such matters.

Figure 1.1 Interest Rates: Italian Major Business Cities (1200–1400)

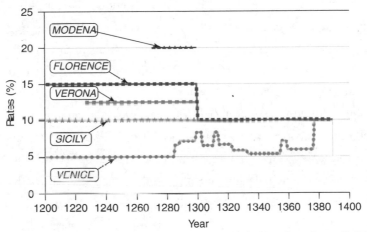

Data Source: Different data for interest rates for Italian cities gained from chapter 9, page 90–101, *A History of Interest Rates*, Fourth Edition, Sidney Homer, Richard Sylla.

Calculations by:
Minjie Zhang, Fall 2011

LEONARDO FIBONACCI (1170–1250)

Historians speculate his *Liber Abaci* was copied and used as the basis for hundreds and possibly thousands of other derivative works during the Middle Ages. These textbooks formed the basic curriculum at so-called *abaci* schools, which taught commercial mathematics and finance to children around southern Europe. Think of them as the forerunners to today's business schools.

Without a doubt, Fibonacci's most lasting contribution to society was his promotion and advocacy of the Hindu–Arabic numeral system as an alternative to Roman numerals for commercial transactions. Oddly enough, this process wasn't as smooth as you might think. Getting merchants to adopt this way of keeping records and calculations wasn't easy. For the most part merchants conducted business with an abacus, some chalk and much hand waving, and they didn't see the need for modern-day numbers. In fact, the rival merchant city of Florence didn't take kindly to this innovation and actually banned (yes, outlawed) use of the so-called new numerals. Even 300 years later, in the middle of the 16th century, merchants in Frankfurt, Germany, had issues with Hindu–Arabic digits and introduced legislation to ban their use in commercial transactions in favor of the more conventional Roman numerals. (Can you believe it? Perhaps the abacus manufacturers lobbied for that one.)

But beyond making life easier by promoting digits and numbers, Fibonacci's contribution to the more specialized field of financial economics has only recently been recognized by historians. For a very long time his work was actually lost, and it was only in the 18th century that it was rediscovered. In other words, although Fibonacci is a household name to today's mathematicians and stock market speculators, there was a 500-year period when his name was almost forgotten.

Okay, Here Come the Rabbits

To most amateur mathematicians, Fibonacci is vaguely known for something called the Fibonacci series (a.k.a Fibonacci numbers). Basically, it's a collection of increasing numbers that go on forever, whose first 11 terms are 0, 1, 1, 2, 3, 5, 8, 13, 21, 34, 55, etc. This sort of thing is called an *infinite series.* Do you see any pattern here? Can you guess the next number in this series? I'll show you momentarily.

As mentioned earlier, Fibonacci's classic book, *Liber Abaci*, includes many diverse questions meant to illustrate the power of the numerical techniques and algorithms he introduced. Among the assortment of commercial and interest-loan problems in one of the advanced chapters was this rather odd problem involving rabbits and sexual reproduction:

How Many Pairs of Rabbits Are Created by One Pair in One Year: A certain man had one pair of rabbits together in a certain enclosed space, and one wishes to know how many are created from the pair in one year when it is the nature in a single month to bear another pair and in the second month those born to bear also . . . (Sigler translation, chapter 12, page 404)

Here is how to think about this whole sordid affair.

A pair of rabbits produces two pairs over the course of their life, one at the end of the first month of their life and then another at the end of the second month of their life, and then they die. Each pair of offspring does exactly the same.

You start with one pair at the beginning, which produces a pair by the end of the first month, leaving a total of two pairs. At the end of the second month the starting pair produces another pair—then dies—plus the pair created by the pair born in month one. So, at the end of the second month, there are three pairs. Then, at the end of the third month, the reproductive process leads to five pairs, resulting in eight pairs by the end of the fourth month, and 13 pairs by the end of month five. Remember that after two months of sexual activity the rabbits die, leaving only their offspring.

Anyway. This is exactly the pattern of numbers I presented above and has become known the world over as the Fibonacci series. Basically, each number in the series is the sum of the previous two numbers. Note that $1 + 2 = 3$, that $2 + 3 = 5$, that $3 + 5 = 8$ and that $5 + 8 = 13$, etc. Back to my earlier question: Can you now figure out the next number in the sequence? After the numbers 34 and 55 comes the number 89—the sum of the two previous numbers. Pretty basic. Then comes 144, then 233, then 377 by the end of the 12 months—quite the number of rabbits. The ratio of two adjacent Fibonacci numbers is 1.618, a.k.a. the Golden Ratio.

Why does this matter? Oddly enough, this question about rabbits, which seems completely *ad hoc* and out of context with the commercial and financial essence of this book, has become *the* most enduring legacy of Fibonacci. The Fibonacci sequence—which people have extended well beyond the first 12 numbers he listed—is more recognized and famous today than his work in popularizing Hindu–Arabic numerals, or even his work in financial mathematics. The Fibonacci series occurs naturally, from flower petals to pineapples, and these numbers have taken on a mystical and even religious role over the centuries. Stock market technicians believe that quoted prices follow Fibonacci sequences, and gamblers swear by Fibonacci when picking cards. Either way, I doubt Fibonacci had any inkling he would be remembered (mostly) for the sexually promiscuous rabbits he introduced on page 404 of *Liber Abaci*.

Fibonacci might be famous for his rabbit series, but his financial contribution to retirement income planning is immortal and of much greater significance.

He Retired Wealthy

In addition to his many scholarly talents, Fibonacci was financially shrewd, politically connected and quite influential in economic matters. His mathematical prowess, and the publication of *Liber Abaci* granted him a private audience with the Holy Roman Emperor, Frederick II, whom he greatly impressed by solving a variety of commercial mathematical problems. Toward the end of Fibonacci's life his fame traveled beyond Pisa, and in 1240, the proud city of his birth issued a proclamation granting him an annual pension of 20 Pisan pounds for life for service to the city. It is not clear whether he spent his retirement years trading stocks using technical analysis, but clearly he didn't run out of money before he ran out of life.

CHAPTER 2

HOW LONG WILL I SPEND IN RETIREMENT?

EQUATION #2: BENJAMIN GOMPERTZ (1779–1865)

$$\ln[p] = (1 - e^{t/b})e^{\left(\frac{x - m}{b}\right)}$$

For a man who never formally attended university, Benjamin Gompertz achieved a level of scientific immortality even the most senior and tenured professors could only dream of today. While most academics toil in obscurity and their names eventually perish despite their frenetic publishing, Gompertz has joined a very small and distinctive group of scholars with an actual equation named after him. The equation has been admired and used by researchers in demographic studies the world over for almost two centuries. His equation might not be as famous as Albert Einstein's ubiquitous $E = MC^2$, but is much more useful for retirement income planning—even if you are a nuclear engineer. Gompertz's claim to fame is the so-called Gompertz law of mortality, depicted above and the subject of this chapter.

Just to be clear, Benjamin Gompertz was not a college dropout who decided to tinker in his parents' garage instead of staying in school. I gather young Benjamin, as an eager teenager, would have loved nothing more than to enroll in university. He just wasn't allowed. You see, back in 1795 England there were strict race and religion-based rules on who could attend university, and he was Jewish—hence, no admission. Gompertz had to make do with an informal "street" education.

Despite these impediments, this self-starter taught himself everything there was to know about mathematics—becoming a virtual expert in, and devotee of, Newtonian physics along the way—making it all the way to the top of British scientific aristocracy. Gompertz was made a Fellow of the Royal Society, and eventually elected president. This honor would certainly be inconceivable in today's hierarchical scientific world where an Oxbridge or Ivy League doctorate and 10 years of schooling are prerequisites.

Simplistic Retirement Planning

In the previous chapter we saw that Fibonacci taught the world how long the money will last. In this chapter we address the natural follow-up question: How long does this money *have* to last? Or, stated differently: How long will you (and/or your partner) live? Whether you have money squirreled away in a tax-sheltered savings account, an investment-based ("Defined Contribution") pension plan or just a piggy bank under your mattress, this money must last for *the rest of your life.* You can see that it's quite senseless to conduct any sort of financial planning without devoting some time to the topic of human longevity.

I've observed that often when financial advisors discuss retirement income planning with their clients, they start by asking questions about how long they would *like* to plan for, or the age to which they *expect* to live, for example age 85 or 90. Consistent with the pick-your-timeline philosophy, many of today's popular Web-based retirement calculators ask users to select a lifetime horizon in advance. All subsequent calculations—Do I have enough? Will the money last?—are based on this preselected lifetime horizon. They all use a variant of Fibonacci's time value of money equation (Equation #1). That's great, but they stop there.

So, for example, using Equation #1 you might be told that if you want your million-dollar nest egg to last to age 85—roughly how long people live—spend no more than $75,000 per year. If you think 85 is too early, you can run the same exercise to age 90 and you'll learn you should spend no more than $60,000 per year, etc. Presumably, you'll shoot yourself if you live beyond the lifetime horizon.

Perhaps you have played with these tools, using various lifetime horizons. I can just hear the discussions: "Aunt Gemma lived to 97, but Uncle Bob only made it to 82, so maybe we should use age 90?" Or "Oh dear, we can only spend $60,000 per year if we plan to 90," which then leads to the inevitable silliness of: "Okay, let's plan only until 85, because we really need $75,000 per year."

The problem with this approach is that you really shouldn't be picking your life horizon in advance. Fibonacci's equation was just the beginning. Life is random, and you know it. In my opinion, the next step in a *scientific approach* to retirement income planning is to understand how random your remaining lifespan really can be. To make an informed decision, you need to know the odds of living to various ages. Then you can decide how long you want to plan for, and—more importantly—how you plan to adjust your spending if you live to a very old age.

This is precisely where Benjamin Gompertz's handy little equation comes in, and why his equation is Equation #2.

Gompertz's Big Discovery

Benjamin Gompertz, like other actuaries, spent much of his research life examining records of death—and specifically the exact ages at which people died. In all likelihood, actuaries are the only people who actually enjoy reading the obituaries in the local newspapers! They use the obituaries to carefully compile tables of ages at which people died, much like the first two columns of Table 2.1, below.

Until Benjamin Gompertz, scientists and researchers—including Edmond Halley, whom you'll learn about in the next chapter—would compile or collect these records, but had never much considered extracting any forward-looking patterns or formal laws of mortality. They knew how many people had died in Carlisle or Northampton in the past and could predict how many might die in the next few years—which was very important for insurance pricing—but the entire activity was rather *ad hoc* in the early 19th century. You could say that the mortality tables compiled by statisticians of the day showed a single frame from a snapshot of the past. Benjamin Gompertz figured out how to convert these individual frames into a movie.

The first two columns of Table 2.1 illustrate a snapshot from a hypothetical life table (also known as a mortality table). You'll see there were 98,585 people aged 45 years and alive in a given (hypothetical) year. Then, of that large group, 146 people died between the ages of 45 and 46, then 161 people died between the ages of 46 and 47, then 177 people died between the ages of 47 and 48, etc. Table 2.1 can be extended by another 50 or so rows—assuming you track this group long enough—all the way until the last person died at age 92 (in this group), at which point the next entry would be zero.

Now, if you casually look at the mortality table you can see the number of people dying tends to increase over time as they age—which is somewhat obvious. At older ages—when very few people in that age category are still alive—one might expect the number of people dying in any given year will also decline. However, the *mortality rate*, defined as the ratio of the number of people who died versus the number alive at the beginning of the year, always increases. It's displayed in column 4 and listed as 0.148% during age 45, then 0.164% during age 46, etc. You can easily reproduce these numbers yourself by dividing 146 (deaths during the year) by 98,585 (the number alive at age 45) or 161 by 98,439 (the number alive at age 46).

That these annual mortality rates increased with age was well documented and understood before Gompertz's time. As I said,

Table 2.1 Tracking a Group of 45-Year-Olds as They Age . . . and Die

Age	Alive at Birthday	Die in Year	Mortality Rate (%)	Nat. Log. of Mortality Rate	Change in Value with Age
45	98,585	146	0.148	−6.615	N.A
46	98,439	161	0.164	−6.416	0.0993
47	98,278	177	0.180	−6.319	0.0964
48	98,101	195	0.199	−6.221	0.0987
49	97,906	214	0.219	−6.126	0.0950
50	97,692	236	0.242	−6.026	0.1000
51	97,456	259	0.266	−5.930	0.0954
52	97,197	285	0.293	−5.832	0.0983
53	96,912	313	0.323	−5.735	0.0967
54	96,599	345	0.357	−5.635	0.1006

these sorts of mortality tables had been compiled by statisticians and demographers for centuries.

But Gompertz went one step further with these numbers in search of a pattern or a natural law. He wanted something like the laws of gravity put forth by his British hero, Sir Isaac Newton. So he tinkered, played with and manipulated the mortality rates from many different mortality tables. Along the way, he decided to compute the logarithm of these numbers. He did this to measure the *rate* at which the mortality *rate* (yes, double rate) was changing over time. The logarithm is the best way to extract these rates.

The *natural* logarithm of the mortality rates—remember that we used this in Chapter One as well—are displayed in the fifth column of the table. Notice that these numbers are all negative because the logarithm of any number smaller than one, is negative. Notice that the values in that column increase with age. The first number is −6.615 and the second number is −6.416, and the third number is −6.319, etc.

Finally, Benjamin Gompertz looked at the differences in values (column 5) between two adjacent ages, and that's when the lightbulb went on!

When he subtracted subsequent values from each other—the logarithm of the mortality rate at age 47 minus the logarithm of the mortality rate at 46, or the logarithm of the mortality rate at age 48 minus the logarithm of the mortality rate at 47, for example—all displayed in the sixth and final column of the table, he got numbers that were almost identical.

As you can see, they are between 9% and 10%, regardless of age! He did this process for many different age blocks, different mortality tables with populations from different cities and countries. Sure, the mortality rates were quite different depending on age, gender, country of origin and city, but the difference in logs was the same.

To Benjamin Gompertz this was a very odd coincidence, and an indication that perhaps something deeper was at work. Why should the difference in the logarithm of death rates be relatively constant with age? In fact, if you plot the values themselves (column 5) they fall on a straight line, with a slope that is approximately 9%. Mathematically speaking, if the difference between the natural logarithm of the mortality rate is constant over time, the mortality rate itself is growing exponentially at the rate of 9% per year.

Benjamin Gompertz deduced there was a law of nature at work. Namely, the rate at which people die grows exponentially over time, which is why the natural logarithm grows linearly. That is, the line you see in the fifth column of Table 2.1. Death was no longer just a random event whose likelihood increased with age: there was an underlying force of mortality that led to these values.

Benjamin Gompertz discovered that your probability of dying in the next year increases by approximately 9% per year, from adulthood until old age. Subsequent bio-demographic research has shown that every species on earth has its own rate.

The Grim Reaper was following a very careful script. He didn't just randomly select some older and a few younger people to kill. Rather, in any given year, he would methodically kill 9% more 46-year-olds than 45-year-olds. In the same year, he would kill 9% more 47-year-olds than 46-year-olds, and 9% more 48-years-olds than 47-year-olds. This death ratio was maintained from the very young to the very old. The Grim Reaper had a quota to maintain and every year the counting would begin anew. Like Isaac Newton's laws of gravity, discovered over a century earlier, death itself obeyed its own immutable law.

The rest is just mathematical manipulations.

The straight line that Gompertz discovered had a slope of approximately 9%, but it also had an intercept. This is the point at which the line meets the axis. In other words, there are two degrees of freedom (or biological inputs) that determine this line. This is why we need two parameters to pin down the Gompertz equation. One determines the rate (i.e., 9%) and the other determines where it all ends.

That is Gompertz's equation, and why it is named after him.

Using the Second Most Important Equation

Now, let us roll up our sleeves and get to work. Equation #2 delivers the natural logarithm of the probability you'll live to any given age. To make sense of and actually use that number, you must undo the natural logarithm by taking its natural exponent. This process is explained in the Appendix and sounds more complicated than it actually is. Really, it's no more elaborate than having prices listed in euros and then converting them into dollars. Or having a thermostat that displays temperature in Fahrenheit, when you are more accustomed to Celsius.

The right-hand side includes four parameters or inputs that give life to the equation and make it useful in different situations. The four parameters are: i) your current age (x, in years); ii) the number of years you might still live (t, in years); iii) the modal value of human life (m, in years); and iv) the dispersion coefficient of human life (b, in years). The first two should be self-evident, the last two not so much. For readers wondering about these last two items and what they mean, take $m = 87.25$ years and $b = 9.5$ years. They are related to the above-mentioned 9% rate, and I'll explain in more detail later, but here's a preview.

Every species—or any homogeneous group within that species, such as healthy, white, female humans—has its own personal m values. The letter m stands for "modal value of life." It is the age at which you are most likely—although obviously not guaranteed—to die. So the entire (heterogeneous) population of Canadians, for example, might be better modeled with a higher m, compared to Americans, for example. In general, a well-trained actuary or medical scientist can give you a more accurate assessment, but in this chapter and book we will stick with $m = 87.25$ years and $b = 9.5$ years, to keep things simple.

A Detailed Example: Different (x) and (t) Values

You should now be ready to get some numbers, forecast the length of your retirement and determine how long the money must last. Let's say you're currently 57—pondering early retirement—and are wondering about the probability or chances you'll live to 90. This is another 33 years of life. In this case, you would use Equation #2 with parameters (i.e., the stuff on the right-hand side) of $x = 57$, $t = 33$ and the above mentioned $m = 87.25$ and $b = 9.5$.

Here we go, step by step. Hang in there, or perhaps take a look at the Appendix before you leap into the pit of es and lns.

Notice that the right-hand side is the product of two independent terms, both involving the natural exponent, e. Remember, in addition to representing the opposite of the natural logarithm, e is actually shorthand notation for the number 2.7183. So $e^2 = 7.389$, obviously $e^1 = 2.7183$ and $e^0 = 1$.

The first term in Equation #2 is $(1-e^{t/b})$ and the second term is $(e^{(x-m)/b})$. In numbers, this is the product of -31.255 and 0.04141, which equals -1.29431. Hang tight, we're almost there. We have the natural logarithm of the probability a 57-year-old will survive to the age of 90 under the Gompertz law of mortality.

Finally, to undo the natural logarithm (Fahrenheit) and get the answer in percentages (Celsius), compute the natural exponent of -1.29431, that is: $2.7183^{-1.29431}$ to arrive at 27.41%. *Voilà.* This is the probability you will survive to 90.

Here it is in words. One in four people who are alive at 57 will be around by the time they are 90.

I will now do this again for another set of numbers. Assuming you are 57 years old, what's the probability you will live to 100 under the Gompertz law of mortality? In this case you should use the same $m = 87.25$ and $b = 9.5$ and $x = 57$ parameter values, but since you're trying to predict survival to 100, 43 years away, you should use the parameter $t = 43$ (instead of 33). In this case the equation tells us to multiply (the first term) -91.417 (instead of -31.255) and the same 0.04141 (since the second term didn't involve the parameter t) for a total of -3.78568. This is the natural logarithm of the probability you will live to 100. Finally, the Fahrenheit to Celsius conversion (i.e., taking the natural exponent) leaves us with $\ln e^{-3.7865} = 2.27\%$, which are pretty slim chances of living to 100. Yes, a small group will make it—there are around 100,000 centenarians alive in the United States and about 5,000 in Canada—but, under the Gompertz law of mortality, the probability is less than 3% for someone aged 57.

Remember, you can't talk about the probability of living to a given age unless you tell me your current age. That's one of the important takeaways from the Gompertz equation.

Here is one final calculation just to make sure you know and are able to use Equation #2. You are (still) $x = 57$ years old. What are the odds of living to age 84.3? (Yes, this seems like an odd age, but you'll see why I picked this in a minute.)

Living to age 84.3 entails living another $t = 27.3$ years. If you plug this number into Equation #2 you should get the product of -16.70212 by 0.04141, which results in -0.69165. Finally, take the natural exponent of that number and the probability of living to age 84.3 is $e^{-0.69165} = 50\%$. Yes, that is exactly 50% and even odds. In fact, there is a special name for age 84.3 (if you are currently 57 years old) and it's called the *median remaining lifetime*. The word median comes from the fact that 50% of people will live to 84.3 (if they are currently 57) and 50% will not. Now you see why I picked this rather odd-looking number. I actually worked my way backward. I tinkered with the equation until I could find a value of t that would result in exactly 50%.

Many More Values

You can generate many different combinations of current age (x) and survival years (t), as shown in the following table. It displays the probability of surviving to 85, 90, 95 and 100—our main quantity of interest—assuming you are currently between 45 and 80. Each one of the numbers in the table is obtained by plugging the relevant parameters into the right-hand side of Equation #2, then undoing the natural logarithm by taking the natural exponent to extract the survival probability. It's a two-stage process, exactly as I explained earlier.

For example, if you are 65 years old (not 57) currently, the probability of living to 85 is exactly 50%, as per Equation #2, with $x = 65$ and $t = 20$. The probability of living to 90 (if you are 65) is approximately 29%; the probability of living to 95 (if you are 65) is 11.5%;

Table 2.2 Your Probability of Living to 85, 90, 95 and 100

Your Current Age	Probability of Living to 85		Probability of Living to 90		Probability of Living to 95		Probability of Living to 100	
	ln[p]	p (%)	ln[p]	p (%)	ln[p]	p (%)	ln[p]	p (%)
45	-0.77741	46.0	-1.32401	26.6	-2.24925	10.5	-3.81538	2.2
50	-0.76930	46.3	-1.31590	26.8	-2.24114	10.6	-3.80727	2.2
55	-0.75557	47.0	-1.30217	27.2	-2.22741	10.8	-3.79354	2.3
60	-0.73233	48.1	-1.27894	27.8	-2.20417	11.0	-3.77030	2.3
65	-0.69299	50.0	-1.23960	29.0	-2.16483	11.5	-3.73097	2.4
70	-0.62641	53.5	-1.17301	30.9	-2.09825	12.3	-3.66438	2.6
75	-0.51370	59.8	-1.06031	34.6	-1.98554	13.7	-3.55168	2.9
80	-0.32292	72.4	-0.86953	41.9	-1.79477	16.6	-3.36090	3.5
85	0.00000	100.0	-0.54661	57.9	-1.47184	23.0	-3.03798	4.8

and the probability of living to 100 (if you are 65) is 2.4%. Notice how I constantly emphasize your current age when displaying the probability of living to any given age. Your current age is part of the equation and it makes no sense to talk about living to age y or z without specifying your current age.

You'll notice that in Table 2.2 I've displayed two columns of numbers for each one of the age-pair combinations. The first number is the natural logarithm of the probability (the proper right-hand side of Equation #2) while the second is the natural exponent of that number (to undo the logarithm), the actual probability everyone is interested in. By now I hope this process is clear. Remember, the logarithm of the mortality rate increases linearly with age, so it should come as no surprise that natural logarithms feature so prominently in the equation.

Taking a broader view of the table, notice that if you are 80 the probability of living an additional five years is much higher than 50%; it's actually 72.4%. Clearly, there's a great chance of making it to 85 if you are already 80, versus someone who is only 65. This—once again—is why it makes little sense to talk about the odds of living to any age without basing the statement on your current age. On the other extreme, the last column of Table 2.2 displays the natural logarithm of the probability of living to 100. Notice how all the numbers in this table—at least from age 45 to 75—are under 3%. They don't change much with your current age. They are quite slim regardless of how old you actually are today. It's only when you get to 85 that these odds start to get close to 5%.

As Gompertz's law says, your mortality rate is increasing by 9% per year, so whether you are 45 or 65, the chances of becoming a centenarian are quite slim.

What About Males versus Females?

You might be wondering why your gender or sex is not included in this important Gompertz equation. After all, aren't females supposed to live longer than males? And for that matter, what about your health? What if your doctor says you're in perfect health versus needs-to-be-improved health? What about genes and DNA? Shouldn't that have an impact as well? And, for that matter, hasn't mortality improved and life expectancies increased since Gompertz's time in the early 19th century?

Yes, yes and yes. The answer is buried in the two parameters m and b—and especially the first m—which I assumed were equal to 87.25 years and 9.5 years, respectively, in the equation. I'll now explain in more detail.

Recall that the main equation required four input variables. The first two (x, t) were your current age and the number of years of life you were trying to forecast. Table 2.2 displayed probabilities for many combinations of these two values. The other two parameters (m, b) are demographic variables that can depend on species, gender, citizenship, health and even wealth. The b was linked to the 9% increase in death rate from the Gompertz discovery, and the m was linked to the age at which people are most likely to die.

As mentioned earlier, I used the numbers $m = 87.25$ and $b = 9.5$ because they're representative of a general (healthy, modern) North American population. These two parameters—and especially the m value—very much depend on the specifics of your situation. For example, if you are a healthy female you should probably use the equation with an additional three to five years added; your personal m should be about 90 or so. On the other hand, if you are male, perhaps take off a few years and use the equation with m being about 85 or so. The same goes for people in really good health versus people in poor health, or citizens of Japan (where life expectancy at birth is about 83 years) versus people in Botswana (where life expectancy at birth is only 58 years). Alas, during Gompertz's time, the m value was quite a bit lower than it is now.

Nevertheless, regardless of what specific values you decide to use for the m parameter, the qualitative result is the same. Your mortality rate increases by something between 8% and 10% per year, with the average being about 9%. Like Newton's gravitation, there is no escaping that law.

Testing the Internal Limits of the Equation

One of the many ways mathematicians test whether an equation is doing what it should and makes intuitive sense is by using very large or very small values for the input parameters—in this case, x, t, m, b—to see what happens to the result. The idea is to make sure your results are consistent with what you might expect, in situations you know. The next few paragraphs might get a bit too mathematical for your palate, so feel free to jump ahead to the next section. But, for those of you who enjoyed smashing toy trucks together as kids, this might be to your taste.

Let's put on our construction hats and try to blow up the equation with some extreme cases. First, let's see what happens when we plug a value of $t = 0$ into Equation #2. In that case, since the natural exponent of zero is one, the right-hand side of Equation #2 is exactly zero. So the natural logarithm of the probability of living for 0 more years is zero. This implies the actual probability of living for 0 more years—or as the Bee Gees would say, staying alive for this instant—is $e^0 = 1$, which is 100%. Does this make sense? It should.

Now let me do the same for a very large (infinite) value of t. Think of the probability of living for 1,000 years (like Methuselah). In this case, the natural exponent of a very large number is a very, very large number, and the right-hand side of Equation #2 becomes $(1 - 1.97 \times 10^{434})\, e^{(x-m)/b} \to \infty$. By the way, the very large number you are multiplying 1.97 by, is the number 10 with 434 zeros after it. So the natural logarithm of the survival probability is very, very negative. The natural exponent—remember Fahrenheit to Celsius—then leads to $e^{-\infty} \to 0$. No surprise here: the probability of catching up to the biblical Methuselah is very, very close to zero.

In fact, here's what Gompertz himself says about this on page 516 in the paper that made him famous:

"Such a law of mortality would indeed make it appear that there was no positive limit to a person's age. But, it would be easy, even in the case of the hypothesis, to show that a very limited age might be assumed to which it would be extremely improbable that any one should have been known to attain . . . "

"And though the limit to the possible duration of life is a subject not likely ever to be determined, even should it exist, still it appears interesting to dwell on a consequence which would follow, should the mortality of old age be as above described . . . Neither profane history nor modern experience could contradict the possibility of the great age of the patriarchs of the scripture . . ."

In other words, according to this law of mortality there's always a chance—miniscule and infinitesimal—that a person could live to any arbitrarily large age. Indeed, Benjamin Gompertz might have been a great scientist, but he was also a religious man.

How Accurate Is This Equation Today?

In less than 15 years—on June 9, 2025, to be precise—the scientific community will celebrate two centuries of the Gompertz law of mortality. And, like anything that has been around for more than 200 years, it's starting to show its age.

Figures 2.1a and b display the ubiquitous line—the natural logarithm of mortality rates—for both the United States and Canada over different periods of time. Figure 2.1a presents the numbers for Canada, and Figure 2.1b for the United States. The mortality rates are for 1950, 1990 and 2007. Notice—as Gompertz discovered—they all fall on a straight line. The line for 1950 is the highest, because mortality rates were higher 50 years ago. The line for 2007 is the lowest, since overall mortality rates have improved since then.

Figure 2.1a Mortality Rates over Age and Time
(Canada: 1950, 1990, and 2007)

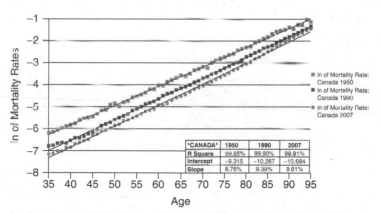

CANADA	1950	1990	2007
R Square	99.85%	99.90%	99.81%
Intercept	−9.315	−10.267	−10.684
Slope	8.76%	9.39%	9.61%

Data Source: Human Mortality Database: UC, Berkeley (U.S.) www.mortality.org (October 2011).

47

Figure 2.1b Mortality Rates over Age and Time
(Canada: 1950,1990 and 2007)

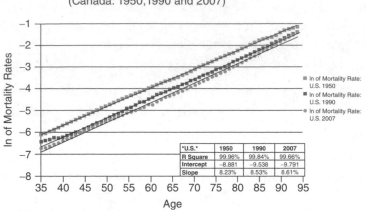

"U.S."	1950	1990	2007
R Square	99.96%	99.84%	99.66%
Intercept	−8.881	−9.538	−9.791
Slope	8.23%	8.53%	8.61%

Legend:
- ln of Mortality Rate: U.S. 1950
- ln of Mortality Rate: U.S. 1990
- ln of Mortality Rate: U.S. 2007

Data Source: Human Mortality Database: UC, Berkeley (U.S.) www.mortality.org (October 2011).

The good news from Figure 2.1a and Figure 2.1b is that *even today* the numbers fall on a straight line whose slope (or rate of increase) is something between 8% and 10% for the entire population, depending on the country and the time period. The bad news is that the pretty picture you see only works between the ages of 35 and about 95. Before and after those ages, the rates don't quite fall on the straight line. And, at advanced ages there are serious problems with the Gompertz law of mortality. Centenarians are especially guilty of breaking that law. I'll get to their lawlessness in a moment.

The recent view of human mortality is that its actual force increases in a random manner with age and over time. Thus, instead of increasing by x% every year, for example, it increases by an *average* of x%, and x itself varies depending on many other latent variables. While these differences might seem rather technical to the non-specialist, they have some important real-world implications.

Note that any law of mortality that claims your probability of death increases by $x\%$ per year obviously ignores freak accidents and other unnatural causes of death. This is something that is quite evident in North America around the age of 18 to 25 when youngsters first learn how to drive. The AIDS epidemic also distorted mortality probabilities, as do wars and plagues. Besides natural biological aging there are other (random) causes of death that may not be related to age or aging.

Even Benjamin Gompertz himself realized this. In 1825 he wrote:

> "It is possible that death may be the consequence of two generally co-existing causes. The one [is] chance, without previous disposition to death or deterioration. The other [is] a deterioration, or an increased inability to withstand destruction . . ."

There's more to death than just a steady 9% upward march in mortality rates. As I alluded to earlier, the (modern) problem with Gompertz's law of mortality—where the equation starts to crack—is when you try applying it to people who are already very, very old. Benjamin Gompertz didn't have access to people in their 90s and beyond because there weren't many around in his time. He had data on life and death from people between the ages of 20 and 80, where his law works quite well. You can't fault Gompertz for not stumbling on this one.

But here's something demographers and actuaries have only discovered recently. If you are 90, 95 or 100 and trying to compute the probability of living to 105, 110 or beyond, the Gompertz equation *underestimates* the chances you'll actually reach these higher ages. Equation #2 is too pessimistic when applied to retirees who are already centenarians. In fact, when mortality tables are compiled for people who died at age 100 and beyond, something remarkable shows up in the data. The mortality rate doesn't increase by 9%, 5% or even 1% per year. It stops increasing altogether! The mortality rate flattens somewhere around 104, and the odds of dying in the next year plateau at about 50%. It doesn't change from year to year. Basically, after the age of 105 or so, it becomes a coin toss. Get to be a super-centenarian and all bets are off! In fact, there are some scientists who claim that not only does aging actually stop—which is what it means for the mortality rate to plateau—it might actually reverse itself. This is called *negative senescence*. But, alas, this is taking me far beyond the mandate of this book.

So How Long Should I Plan for in Retirement?

One thing should be absolutely clear: your remaining lifetime is a random variable. It is impossible to predict with certainty how long you will live. As you saw in Table 2.2, for a typical 65-year-old there's a declining probability of living to any given age. The challenge for you—when confronted with this uncertainty—is how to plan for the rest of your life. Would you rather spend more early in retirement, when you're much more likely to be alive, or would you rather spend less but ensure you have enough if you reach 95 or 100? Some people might be willing to reduce their standard of living if they reach an advanced age—which, remember, offers a small chance—while others are not willing to take the risk.

I'll return to this economic tradeoff—spend more today, and per-haps cut back tomorrow—when I introduce and explain Equation #4 and Irving Fisher's contribution in Chapter Four. For now, please keep the following in mind: given the relatively small probability you will actually live to 95 or 100, you might want to consider buying insurance that pays off if you actually reach that age so that you don't have to worry about it for the first 20 years of your retirement. This is a sort of delayed pension, which is a topic I'll return to in the next chapter.

Back to Benjamin Gompertz

Benjamin Gompertz's discovery is the recognition that mortality rates increase exponentially with age, which is why Equation #2 is named after him. And yet, some readers might be surprised to learn that— like Fibonacci—Gompertz never actually wrote down the famous equation bearing his name. In fact, the 70-page paper he wrote and presented to the Royal Society of London in 1825 doesn't include any analytic expression for the survival probability. Alas, like many of the other equations I'll present in the next few chapters—and many other famous centuries-old equations—the author of this equation was more likely to describe it in words rather than algebraic symbols. As well, the notation and terminology used in the time of the inventor—in this case Benjamin Gompertz—was quite different from the language used today. (He was a fan of Isaac Newton's fluxional notation for calculus, which has long fallen out of favor.) So although Gompertz wrote down a mathematical expression for the intensity of mortality—what we call the *mortality rate*—he never quite presented an equation for the survival probability based on his law of mortality. That said, though it took a while for his groundbreaking idea to catch on, fame did come—eventually.

It was a fellow actuary by the name of William Makeham, a younger contemporary of Gompertz, who helped formalize and mathematize the Gompertz law of mortality. Some might say it was William Makeham who turned Benjamin Gompertz into an actuarial rock star.

As you can imagine, Benjamin's skills and insights were extremely valuable to insurance companies in the business of selling life insurance. With an actual equation for mortality and survival rates, companies could do a much better job of computing premiums, setting reserves and managing risk.

You shouldn't be surprised to learn Benjamin Gompertz was hired as the chief actuary at one of the largest insurance companies in England, the Alliance Assurance Company—a company founded by his brother-in-law, Sir Moses Montefiore, together with the famous Nathan Rothschild of the Rothschild banking dynasty—where he served for almost three decades. He also became a full member of the London Stock Exchange (LSE) at 30 while retaining active involvement in the Astronomical Society. To all who came into contact with him, Gompertz was a true scholar, gentleman and successful businessman.

According to his obituary, he was born on March 5, 1779, in London and died on July 14, 1865, in London, at the age of 86—which is exactly what one might expect under the Gompertz law of mortality.

CHAPTER 3

IS A PENSION ANNUITY WORTH IT?

EQUATION #3: EDMOND HALLEY (1656–1742)

$$a_x = \sum_{i=1}^{\infty} \frac{{}_iP_x}{(1+R)^i}$$

Toward the end of the 17th century, politicians and bureaucrats in London, England, were facing a problem not unlike that faced by many aging cities in the early 21st century. For years, they had made promises to pay lifetime pensions to the city's residents, but hadn't bothered to properly estimate what those liabilities were worth or how much they should set aside to pay pensions. Using today's modern financial terminology, they had large unfunded off-balance sheet liabilities, which they were fairly ignorant about. In the same vein, insurance companies were selling individual annuities to people of all ages but were charging them a flat, fixed price regardless of how old or how young they were.

In fact, various kings and queens were in the habit of borrowing money from their loyal subjects, with a promise to pay them back a lifetime pension, but had similarly never bothered to set aside or compute reserves to make those payments. According to some historians, the French treasury issued life annuities (*rentes viagères*) instead of regular bonds at extremely generous yields that were the same for young and old alike. It is said that this led to the treasury's ultimate bankruptcy prior to the French Revolution.

Anyway, the challenge of properly pricing and valuing a life annuity took on greater visibility during the 1670s and '80s, and various scholars were asked to opine on the matter.

One reason this problem was more vexing than you might expect is that mortality patterns as a function of age had never been studied carefully. Remember, this was more than 150 years before Benjamin Gompertz, our hero from Chapter Two, came on the scene and formalized a law of mortality. And while some early demographers (such as John Gaunt) tried to collect data on population distributions, the immigrant and transitory nature of London's population made it almost impossible to estimate age-dependent mortality rates in a precise manner. Basically, the creation of life tables using a closed population was out of the question for the vibrant and bustling metropolis that was London, England, in the late 17th century.

Against this backdrop, in early 1690, the Royal Society (think of it as a supreme council of scientists) asked a young and confident scientist by the name of Edmond Halley to help out. Halley attacked this problem in a rather novel way, made actuarial history and came up with the first formal expression for the value of a *pension annuity*. Yes, that's the astronomer Edmond Halley with the famous comet named after him.

The astronomer Edmond Halley was a mere 35 years old when he tackled the pricing of individual annuities, but was already widely known and respected in scientific circles around England and beyond. He had traveled widely, participated in scientific expeditions, published prolifically and was actually something of a social celebrity as well.

Edmond Halley, via the Royal Society, obtained some unique demographic data from a place very far from London. In particular, he selected the city of Breslau, (in modern-day Poland), where the population was large enough—but not as transient and consequently challenging to measure—and he created the first table documenting lives, deaths and mortality rates.

Halley wrote a famous article, eventually published in 1693 by the Royal Society in its *Philosophical Transactions*, where he displayed the first reliable life table and summarized his thinking about mortality rates as a function of age. Most importantly for the purposes of this book, he laid down the foundations for determining what a pension annuity is worth, leading to Equation #3.

Why a famous astronomer who spent his time gazing at stars and comets in far-flung observatories around the world would have accepted the task and delve enthusiastically into tackling a rather morbid problem of determining mortality rates is rather puzzling. One can speculate that Halley's sudden interest in death might have been kindled by the fact that his father—also called Edmond Halley, a wealthy aristocrat and businessman—was alleged to have been involved in the Rye House Plot. For those readers who are not English history buffs, this was a plot to kill King Charles II and his brother

James in April 1683. To make a long story short, the king and his heir were spared and the conspirators caught, tried and mostly executed, except for those who committed suicide. It's not clear if Halley Sr. was involved in any way, but he was a known associate of some of those involved and was found dead, likely murdered and completely naked except for his shoes, floating in a local river in April 1684.

I'll return later to that story and the problems it caused Halley Jr., the astronomer.

Take the Pension or a Lump Sum?

Nowadays, most large employers around the world—whether in the public or private sector—offer some sort of *retirement savings plan* to their workforce in which money is set aside for existing employees when they retire. These plans include fairly large sums of money that are often invested in stocks, bonds, real estate and other financial instruments. The funds inside the plan grow over time as a result of: i) contributions by the employer and the employee to the savings plan, and ii) the performance of the plan's individual investments. Collectively, and globally, there are trillions of dollars sitting inside retirement plans, and it's not uncommon for large employers to have hundreds of billions of dollars in just one plan. At retirement, or upon separation from the employer, the employee is entitled to a very small piece of this very large pot. It is his/her retirement nest egg.

Now, although I've just described the common features of *all* retirement savings plans, there are two completely different ways a retiring employee can access his/her slice of the pension pie. Some pension plans *guarantee a monthly payment* for the rest of your life, while the others *only offer a lump sum of money*. If your particular plan guarantees you an income during retirement, it's called a Defined

Benefit (DB) plan. But if all the plan offers is a non-guaranteed sum of money, it's called a Defined Contribution (DC) plan. The emphasis—and most important word—is *guaranteed*. Some plans promise their workers something (DB), while other (DC) plans offer projections, hopes and expectations, but they promise you nothing.

To make things slightly more complicated, any DB pension plans promising an income for the rest of your life actually offer you the option to walk away from the plan when you retire, with a lump sum. And, although DC plans promise you nothing but the slice of a pie, many have recently begun offering the option of selecting a pension annuity when you retire. This can all get confusing, but it doesn't change the fundamental mechanics of the plan while you're still working. To get some clarity around this, ask your plan administrator the following: Is anything guaranteed? If the answer is "no," then you're probably in a DC plan. If the answer is "yes," you're likely in a DB plan.

While at first glance you might think having something guaranteed (think DB) is better than having a pension that's not guaranteed (think DC), the devil is in the details. For example, at retirement would you rather get a lifetime pension annuity of $1,000 per month, or a lump sum of $300,000? Are you better off taking the money out of your employer's pension plan and trying to bake your own pension at home? Or, would you rather get $1,000 per month for the rest of your life, or $750 per month for the rest of *either your or your spouse's life*? These are some tough questions people face as they near retirement, and precisely where Edmond Halley's pension annuity equation is really handy.

Basically, his equation tells you what the lifetime pension that most DB pension plans offer when you retire is really worth. Along

Table 3.1 Retirement Plan Pension Choices

	Take It as a Lump Sum	Select a Life Annuity
1) Overall flexibility	You can invest the money any way you want, and spend more or less money over time.	Plan sponsor manages the money, but sends you a fixed monthly check, like a salary.
2) Guarantees and promises	Unless you buy some protection, you are at the mercy of the market.	Income for the rest of you and your spouse's life that can't be outlived. A form of insurance.
3) Legacy value	Funds can be bequeathed or transferred, and are part of the retiree's estate.	Possibly reduced income for spouse upon death, nothing left for the next generation.
4) Decision complexity	You must manage the money for the rest of your life, or delegate the responsibility.	Once the initial decision is made, no further decisions are required. Low complexity.
5) Inflation protection	Depends on how you invest the money, and the type of investments you select.	Some employers provide income adjusted annually for inflation, but most do not.
6) Credit safety	Assuming the money is invested in conventional funds, there is no great risk.	You are at the mercy of the pension plan sponsor, and their ultimate guarantor.
7) Health implications	If the couple is in (very) poor health, taking the lump sum is a (much) better option.	Pension income partially dies with you, and completely dies with your spouse. A gamble.

the same lines, it tells you what it would cost to buy a pension annuity from an insurance company when you retire, if you happen to be in a DC plan that doesn't offer one. It's a really handy equation that's indispensable for anyone trying to decide: "Should I take the lump sum or the pension annuity?"

The tradeoffs you face between taking the pension lump sum at retirement or opting for the pension annuity are summarized and displayed in Table 3.1.

For example, if you're in poor health you might want to elect to take the lump sum. If you think you are healthier than everyone else, then go for the pension annuity. If you want to leave money to the kids and grandkids, go for the lump sum. But if you're concerned about not having enough money to live on for the rest of your life, go for the pension. If you are concerned about managing, investing and allocating your money well into your old age, take the pension annuity. But if you feel comfortable and competent enough to do your own investing, or you have a trusted advisor, go for the lump sum.

These are all big-picture decisions you must make that are quite independent of the numbers and figures. But, when it finally comes time to compare values and decide, Halley's equation, Equation #3, is indispensable.

In sum, having an equation to figure out what a pension annuity is worth, or what it might cost to buy one, is clearly one of the most important retirement issues to contemplate. For many retirees, it's the single most important decision they face.

Halley's History, Part I

Entire books have been written about Edmond Halley, and almost every aspect of his scientific life has been well documented. The copious amounts of available information about Halley's social interactions stands in contrast to the hero of Chapter One, Leonardo Fibonacci.

At the same time, it becomes difficult to summarize Halley's life's work in a few mere paragraphs.

To astronomers and geophysicists, Edmond Halley is a celebrity, an Elvis Presley of the Renaissance. Like Elvis, Halley continues to be cited long after his time. Edmond Halley's titles were numerous. He was the Astronomer Royal, the King's personal astronomer. His academic title was the Savilian Professor of Geometry at Oxford University. He was the world's first geophysicist, but also a military engineer, physical geographer and surveyor. He published a detailed catalogue of the stars in the southern sky, and was even an expert on trade winds and monsoons. He created the first known map of the earth's magnetic fields, today called Halleyan lines in his honor.

Halley was also a superb seaman, navigator and explorer. As a scientist, he not only went on lengthy maritime expeditions around the world, he actually *commanded* them and was a temporary captain in the Royal Navy.

And yet, his greatest claim to scientific fame might not be his recurring comet—which I promise to return to later—or even his famed pension annuity equation, but rather his part in publishing the most famous scientific book ever: Isaac Newton's *Principles*. Sir Isaac Newton was a genius and a giant, but not very wealthy or organized. It was Edmond Halley who motivated and assisted Newton in publishing the book which changed science forever. He was Newton's editor, his publisher—as the Clerk of the Royal Society—and apparently the private banker who financed its publication. To many historians of science, Newton wouldn't have been possible without Halley. Then again, Halley's comet and astronomical calculations wouldn't have been possible without Newton.

The Third Equation, Explained

As you probably noticed from the header at the beginning of this chapter, Equation #3 doesn't quite look like the simple ones from the first two chapters. To make sense of everything, let's go through the components of Equation #3 step by step.

First, on the far left-hand side there's a new symbol most readers probably haven't seen before: a_x, denoting the value of a $1-per-year-for-life (ordinary) pension annuity for someone currently x years old. This is often called the *pension annuity factor* in the pension industry. Think a_{60} for a 60-year-old, or a_{65} for a 65-year-old or a_{92} for a 92-year-old, to give some examples. The notation might seem odd and awkward, but I didn't make up these symbols. Just to be clear, Edmond Halley did not use these symbols either. The notation was invented— and agreed upon—by actuaries more than a century ago, in the late 1880s.

Let's look at an example of how it works. If $a_{60} = \$20$, the equation essentially says that a 60-year-old should pay $20 for a pension that pays $1 per year, starting immediately, for the rest of his/her life. That pension annuity factor can be scaled up or down so that if you want $12,000 per year, or $1,000 per month, you should pay $20 \times 12 \times 1,000 = \$240,000$ upfront. Think of it as an exchange rate between money today and the promise of income for the rest of your life. The exchange rate can be used in either direction: yen to euro or euro to yen. Give a pension or insurance company $240,000 at age 60, and you'll be entitled to a pension of $1,000 per month. Or vice versa: if your pension plan is offering you a lifetime pension of $1,000 you might be able to get a lump sum value of $240,000. All this is hypothetical, of course, but hopefully you understand what is meant by the symbol a_x. That is the left-hand side of Halley's equation.

Now let's move on to the right-hand side.

That term is the summation from zero (today) to infinity, or the maximum theoretical length of life. The sum is of the survival probability (which you should be familiar with from Chapter Two) divided by the present value factor (which you should be familiar with from Chapter One). If you can evaluate this sum then you'll obtain your annuity factor. In practice, you stop adding terms well before infinity. You will see how in a moment.

The right-hand side of Equation #3 is actually the way Halley himself explained it (verbally) back in 1693:

> On this depends the valuation of annuities upon lives; for it is plain that the purchaser ought to pay for only such a part of the value of the annuity as he has chances that he is living; and this ought to be computed yearly, and the sum of all those yearly values being added together, will amount to the value of the annuity for the life of the person proposed. Now the present value of money payable after a term of years at any given rate of interest, either may be had from the table already computed . . . (Halley, 1693, page 602)

Here it is, in slightly more modern English.

Buying a pension or pension annuity from an insurance company entitles you to a series of periodic payments, similar to a coupon-bearing bond sold by governments and corporations worldwide. The value of the pension annuity must be lower than the corresponding coupon bond because—as Halley points out—there's a chance you won't live to receive those later payments. Thus, according to Halley, you should pay for a portion "as he has chances of living." This is precisely why you see a survival probability ($_ip_x$) in the numerator of Equation #3. In the denominator you have the present value factor, which converts money payable in the future to units of money payable today. And, although Edmond Halley didn't thank or reference Leonardo Fibonacci's concept of present value—there's a good chance he'd never heard of him—Halley's equation wouldn't have been possible without it. Note, however, that Halley himself used an estimated table of survival probability values rather than an analytic equation like the one developed by Benjamin Gompertz, which was more than a century away from seeing the light of day.

The Third Equation, Demonstrated

The following tables should help you understand how Halley's equation works and can be used in practice. There are three ingredients or input values needed to price a pension annuity, or to figure out its probable worth. The first ingredient is the likelihood of survival to any given age. The second ingredient is the present value factor, which converts future dollars into dollars today, and the third and final ingredient is the amount of the cash flow—that is, the amount of the pension check. These three ingredients are presented in three columns in Table 3.2a, where I've valued a pension of $1 per year for someone who is currently 65 years old and about to retire. To avoid a very long and messy table, I have listed the five-year intervals from age 70 onwards. Notice the declining probabilities of survival, starting with 93.6% for age 70, then 83.6% to age 75, etc. These numbers come from Equation #2, with $m = 87.25$ and $b = 9.5$, although Halley himself has his own set of survival probability numbers from the city of Breslau. The next column displays the present value (today, at 65) of $1 to be received in five, 10, 15 or more years, assuming an annual percentage rate (APR) of 7% with continuous compounding, leading to an effective rate of 7.25%.

Just to ensure this is clear, what I'm saying is that if you have 70 cents and invest it for five years at 7.25% effectively, it will grow to $1 by the end of five years. This is what I mean by present value.

We're almost done. Column C displays the cash flow amount to be received at those five-year milestones, in this case $5. Remember, in this particular example I assumed the pension is paying $5 every five years, rather than $1 every year. The arithmetic is more cumbersome, but the idea's the same. And, if your pension annuity is $100, $1,000 or $10,000, you'd use those numbers in column C instead.

Finally, multiplying the three columns together and then summing them up at the very bottom of the table, Halley's equation leaves us with a pension value of $7.53 at age 65. This, again, is assuming that the interest rate (APR) is 7%. The $7.53 is precisely what pops out of the far right-hand side of Equation #3, where eight terms are added together to produce the pension value.

Here it is again.

If you're exactly 65 years old and have $7.53 to spare, it will buy you a pension that pays $1 per year, or more precisely $5 at the end of every five years. The ratio between up-front cost and annual income is 7.53 to 1. Hopefully at this point you should be able to reproduce and use this equation, without getting bogged down with very long series of numbers.

Now, remember, this was a rather odd pension that paid $5 every five years rather than $1 every year. I did this to save some space (and calculation time), but the same principle would apply if I made those

Table 3.2a What Does a Retirement Pension Cost at Age 65? . . .
When Interest Rates Are 7%

Live to Age	(A) Probability (%)	(B) PV of $1	(C) Cash Flow ($)	A x B x C Product ($)
70	93.6	$ 0.705	5	3.296
75	83.6	$ 0.497	5	2.075
80	69.1	$ 0.350	5	1.208
85	50.0	$ 0.247	5	0.617
90	29.0	$ 0.174	5	0.252
95	11.5	$ 0.122	5	0.070
100	2.4	$ 0.086	5	0.010
105	0.2	$ 0.061	5	0.001
		SUM:		$ 7.530

cash flows weekly, monthly or annually. You multiply probabilities by present values and cash flows and add them up. With a spreadsheet this is a cinch; Table 3.3 provides additional examples, but Edmond Halley did it all by hand!

As you might imagine, the pension's value is quite sensitive to the interest rate (number) used in column C. Under a 7% annual interest rate, the value of the pension is $7.53 at age 65. But what if interest rates are much lower (as they are, for example, in the current economic environment)? The second table, Table 3.2b, does the exact same calculation—which you should be able to reproduce —under a 1% annual percentage rate. In this case columns A and C do not change, but column B (the present value of $1) is much higher compared to Table 3.2a. Notice the number $0.951 in Table 3.2b versus $0.705 in Table 3.2a.

You might have observed the same phenomena, but in a completely different context. Think of what happens to government bond

Table 3.2b What Does a Retirement Pension Cost at Age 65? . . .
When Interest Rates Are 1%

Live to Age	(A) Probability (%)	(B) PV of $1	(C) Cash Flow ($)	A x B x C Product ($)
70	93.6	$ 0.951	5	4.450
75	83.6	$ 0.905	5	3.782
80	69.1	$ 0.861	5	2.972
85	50.0	$ 0.819	5	2.047
90	29.0	$ 0.779	5	1.127
95	11.5	$ 0.741	5	0.425
100	2.4	$ 0.705	5	0.084
105	0.2	$ 0.670	5	0.006
		SUM:		**$ 14.893**

prices when the central bank decides, unexpectedly, to raise interest rates. Usually, the bond market and bond prices drop quite sharply in value. This is a manifestation of the same inverse relationship. Prices go up when interest rates decline and vice versa.

Interest rates make a huge difference, which also explains why pension annuities are much more expensive and costly when rates are abnormally low, as they have been thus far in the early 21st century, compared to a decade or two ago when interest rates were closer to 7%. In fact, Edmond Halley himself used a 6% interest rate when he produced annuity factor tables based on his formula back in 1693.

A Few More Captivating Details

Skip ahead if you want, but there are some *technical issues* you should know about Halley's equation, Equation #3, before you rush out and use it for shopping or price comparison—issues Halley himself would be surprised to learn.

Remember that my objective in presenting Halley's annuity equation was to give you the opportunity to use your own numbers— perhaps different ages or interest rates—and get your own results. That said, the equation will only give you an estimate, and sometimes a very bad one. Let me explain why.

Adverse Selection

Here's a curious fact, little known outside the world of actuarial science. It seems that people who voluntarily purchase life annuities actually live longer than the rest of the population. In fact, there is almost a five-year gap between how long annuitants live, as a group, versus the rest of the population. There are two reasons why this might be the case. First, people who believe they will live longer and are optimistic about their own longevity are more likely to voluntarily purchase annuities. Second, and perhaps more farfetched, as Jane Austen wrote in her book *Sense and Sensibility*, "People always live forever when there is an annuity to be paid them." There might be something that actually keeps them alive. At a basic level, it might be that they can actually afford better health care, or perhaps they don't have to worry about income, but something about lifetime income keeps them alive longer. So Halley's equation—or an online calculator version based on his equation—might tell you a particular annuity would cost $100,000, based on population mortality rates. But there's a good chance if you actually visit an insurance company and ask to buy the same annuity they'll charge you 10% to 20% more because of what I just described, called *adverse selection*.

Group Pricing

The prices of individual annuities, purchased privately by individuals, cost more than group annuities bought for a large group of people at the same time. So while buying in bulk—$1 million versus $100,000—may not get you any discounts, it seems bringing your friends will result in a better deal. Now, it may not be practical or even possible to get your friends to sign up for life annuities, but large employers take advantage of this. In fact, this is why the annuity that might be offered to you from your employer is a much better deal than going out and buying the same cash-flow stream in the open market. Keep this in mind if you're offered a lump sum versus a pension annuity from your employer. You might be getting a better deal than Edmond Halley might have envisioned.

Real versus Nominal

Some pensions pay in real (inflation adjusted) dollars, others pay in nominal (non-inflation-adjusted) dollars. The equations are similar. The prices are not. For example, if your particular pension annuity pays $1,000 per month adjusted for inflation it's obviously much more valuable compared to one that also pays $1,000 per month but is not adjusted for inflation. To estimate exactly how much more the former is versus the latter, you'd use Equation #3 but with an inflation-adjusted interest rate, as opposed to a nominal interest rate. This gets messy with cost-of-living-adjusted pension annuities, which give you a raise each year but don't necessarily protect you against inflation.

The main message here is that all these situations and cases can be handled by suitable modifications of the same equation. Halley still rules.

Pension Value: Age and Interest

Although Equation #3 is relatively easy to use within a spreadsheet program, I will now present a table of these values under a variety of retirement ages and assumed interest rates so readers can develop better intuition for the value of a pension annuity. Unlike the crude calculations in Table 3.2, I assumed an individual who is receiving a total of $1 per year, paid weekly (1/52), whose mortality obeys the Gompertz law described in Chapter Two. Recall, again, that Halley himself used mortality tables from the city of Breslau, and an interest rate of 6%, so his prices were slightly different.

Here's how to read the table.

If you are 60 years old, for example, thinking of taking early retirement, and would like to purchase a pension annuity, when interest rates are at 3% the pension annuity would cost $16.21 per yearly dollar of lifetime income. This number comes from Equation #3 in which the current age $x = 60$ and $r = 0.03$ and the values of $(_ip_{60})$ come from the Gompertz equation, Equation #2. What this means is that if you want $1,000 per month, or $12,000 per year of pension income, you must pay $12,000 \times $16.21 = $194,520. And if interest rates are at 2%, the pension annuity factor (according to Table 3.3) is $18.23 and the $12,000 annual pension will cost you $218,760.

As you can see from the table, if you wait to purchase your pension annuity until a later age, it will be cheaper, although your income will only start at a later age. Likewise, if interest rates move up, your pension will also become cheaper to acquire. By now, this should all be intuitive.

Here's yet another application of Equation #3 and the corresponding table.

EDMOND HALLEY (1656–1742)

Table 3.3 What Is a Pension Annuity Worth? Guaranteed $1 per year for the rest of your life.

Age →	55	60	65	70	75	80	85
Interest Rate (%)							
0	$ 28.01	$ 23.60	$ 19.44	$ 15.59	$ 12.13	$ 9.13	$ 6.63
1	$ 24.03	$ 20.66	$ 17.35	$ 14.18	$ 11.23	$ 8.58	$ 6.32
2	$ 20.83	$ 18.23	$ 15.58	$ 12.95	$ 10.42	$ 8.09	$ 6.03
3	$ 18.23	$ 16.21	$ 14.07	$ 11.88	$ 9.70	$ 7.63	$ 5.77
4	$ 16.10	$ 14.52	$ 12.78	$ 10.94	$ 9.06	$ 7.22	$ 5.52
5	$ 14.34	$ 13.09	$ 11.67	$ 10.12	$ 8.48	$ 6.84	$ 5.29
6	$ 12.87	$ 11.87	$ 10.70	$ 9.39	$ 7.96	$ 6.50	$ 5.08
7	$ 11.63	$ 10.83	$ 9.86	$ 8.74	$ 7.49	$ 6.18	$ 4.88
8	$ 10.59	$ 9.94	$ 9.13	$ 8.16	$ 7.07	$ 5.89	$ 4.69

Imagine you're 70 years old and entitled to a pension annuity of $3,000 per month starting immediately. Further assume your employer offers you a lump-sum payment of $306,000 now, instead of the pension annuity. So should you take the money or keep the pension? This sort of dilemma is faced by hundreds of thousands of people each year, as they approach retirement. Earlier in this chapter I discussed the pros and cons of pension annuities versus managing the money yourself. But here's how to address the financial aspects. Equation #3 should be your guide, and here's how: the $3,000 monthly pension represents $36,000 annually. The $306,000 you're being offered (bribed) to walk away with is exactly 306/36 or 8.5 times the annual income. Now, look at the column under age 70 in Table 3.3. You'll see the value of 8.5 is in between the interest rate of 7% ($8.74) and 8% ($8.16).

What does this mean?

Well, the $306,000 the company is offering you to forfeit the pension is a good deal, only if interest rates in the marketplace are higher than 7.5%. Under those conditions you're getting a fair deal.

But, if market interest rates are at 6% or 5% or even lower (as they are right now), you aren't getting a very good deal; they should have offered you a larger lump sum—and you're probably better off taking the pension annuity (period) payments. And, if the $3,000 monthly pension is inflation-adjusted or cost-of-living-adjusted, there's even more reason *not* to take the lump sum. Of course, this is just part of the analysis of what to do with your pension nest egg at retirement and many other factors should be considered. But hopefully you can see how to use Halley's equation, Equation #3.

For sake of example, here's one final case.

Imagine your employer (on a pension plan) offered you a choice between a lump sum of $500,000 and a lifetime pension of $4,000 per month starting at 65, retirement age. Is that a good deal? The (rough) answer is as follows. If you divide the $500,000 by the annualized $48,000 pension income, you get 10.42 as the implied annuity factor. This is between the $10.70 and $9.86 corresponding to age 65 in Table 3.3. So you're getting between 6% and 7% implicitly from the pension annuity, which is higher than current interest rates. A good deal, I think.

Reality, of course, is more complicated because some pensions are adjusted for inflation, in which case the $4,000 per month mentioned in the last paragraph is really a good deal. In other cases the pension income continues to a surviving spouse—and Halley's equation must be modified slightly—in which case, again, $4,000 is a great deal. On the other hand, if the company offering you the pension income is in financial distress (think airlines, automakers, or steel companies in the 1980s), meaning it may default on your pension, then I'd take the lump sum and run far, far away. Obviously, these are all complications that must be dealt with carefully and with professional advice. But you can never get away from Halley's equation (#3), which is why it's one of the seven most important equations for retirement.

As I mentioned, Halley himself—writing in the 1690s—performed his calculations and displayed results like those in the above table using an interest rate of 6%. His annuity prices at age 55 were 8.51 units, and at age 65 they were 6.54 units. He actually called them "years purchase," the nomenclature at the time, and they are lower than those in Table 3.3. This, of course, is because Breslau in 1690— the source of Halley's mortality estimates—is quite different than North America in 2012. For one, we're much healthier, which reduces mortality rates, and—according to Equation #3—should increase the annuity price. It all works out.

In fact, the 6% interest rate Halley used in the equation was quite typical for the times. According to the Bank of England (displayed in Figure 3.1), interest rates in England around the late 17th century

Figure 3.1 Bank of England Base Rate (Year 1600–2010)

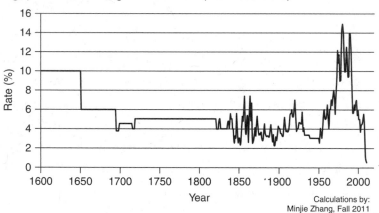

Calculations by:
Minjie Zhang, Fall 2011

Data Source: Bank of England, http://www.bankofengland.co.uk/statistics/index.htm.

were 6%. No doubt if Halley performed his calculations in the economic environment of the late 1970s—a period of high inflation and high interest rates—he would have used the shockingly high 14% rate.

I'll end with a word of warning. Halley's equation and the corresponding values displayed in Table 3.3 are a great start to an important discussion about the value of pensions and annuities, and roughly what such a thing might be worth in the real world. The equation tells you what influences prices, the direction in which they're likely to move over time, as well as the impact of age. But if you really want to know what a pension costs, check out the market prices. In other words, pick up the phone and speak to an agent or broker.

Here is a lesson that goes far beyond retirement planning. When there's a conflict between a model equation value and a market price—the two are saying different things—then side with the market price. There's a long list of hedge funds that learned this particular lesson the hard way.

Back to Halley's History, Part II

Edmond Halley had a financially privileged and quite comfortable life. His family's wealth enabled him to dedicate his time and energies to scientific pursuits, and he didn't have to worry about working for a living.

Even his remunerated work, for the Royal Society as a clerk, was not paid in cash or currency. In fact, he was paid with copies of a (stinker of a) book called *The History of Fish*, which the Royal Society had incurred great debts in publishing a few years earlier, only to be left with much unsold inventory. Only a wealthy (and dedicated) man can afford to work for books (about fish).

His wife, Mary Tooke, whom he married in 1682, came from a well-to-do and successful family associated with the well-known (at the time, at least) Levant Company, which provided the scientist with yet another source of steady income.

Some have claimed Halley's academic career was hindered by his atheism, which has been offered as an explanation for why it took him so long to get a (tenured) university position at Oxford at age 47. In fact, there are stories of Sir Isaac Newton berating Edmond Halley about his "talking ludicrously about religion."

Halley's family life wasn't without strife and stress. At a young age, his natural mother died, leaving him in the care of nannies and family members. His father, Edmond Halley, Sr., remarried after the death of his first wife, Edmond's mother. But the esteemed Edmond Halley, Jr., and his new stepmother didn't get along very well, and he was practically banished from the family home, although—as noted earlier—he still received financial support.

When Edmond Halley, Sr., disappeared in early March 1684, the relationship between Edmond Halley, Jr., and his stepmother soured to the point of recriminations and accusations of infidelity. Indeed, soon after Edmond Halley, Sr., was found dead, the stepmother remarried and she and her stepson ended up in court fighting over the estate's proceeds. Edmond Sr. had left no will or testament, but assets worth millions of English pounds in today's currency.

The circumstances surrounding the death of Edmond Halley, Sr., remain a mystery to this day, with some arguing that he committed suicide—perhaps out of fear of his involvement in a lurid royal plot?—and the police claiming he was murdered by petty thieves.

One thing's sure: the stress around the death of his father and the lawsuits against his stepmother distracted Edmond Halley, Jr., from his astronomical research and he did very little formal work around that time. The one thing he did—in marked contrast to all his other work—was write a paper about pricing life and death, by computing insurance and annuity values. Perhaps mortality was on his mind.

The Great Comet

Like Leonardo Fibonacci and his infamous infinite rabbit series, Edmond Halley is best known for the comet that bears his name—despite his many other and arguably more important accomplishments. His is a peculiar type of fame. Every 75 years or so, there's a flurry of interest in Edmond Halley, then it dissipates. The most recent outburst of notoriety was in 1986. In fact, the New York Times published a special issue to commemorate the comet and remind the world of Halley's achievements.

In brief, the story of the naming of the comet is as follows.

While on an expedition in 1682, Halley observed a very large and striking comet, which he eventually studied using many of the techniques he'd learned from Isaac Newton. Halley went on to conjecture the 1682 comet was the same one seen in 1607 and 1531, and that it would reappear again around 1759. At the time it was a dubious claim and few people thought it was the same comet every time. Technically, he argued some comets had elliptical orbits around the sun (which means they would return, eventually) as opposed to parabolic orbits.

Alas, Edmond Halley was correct but died in January 1742, missing the evidence to support and confirm his predictions. In fact, the return of the comet in 1759 was quite a big deal scientifically since it also offered vindication for Isaac Newton's theories. The world community of astronomers named the comet in Halley's honor, a distinction that has remained ever since.

Halley's comet has had quite a profound impact on certain people over the years. The great American writer and satirist known by his pen name, Mark Twain (his real name was Samuel L. Clemens), said the following, according to his biographer. "*I came in with Halley's Comet in 1835. It is coming again next year, and I expect to go out with it. It will be the greatest disappointment of my life if I don't go out with Halley's Comet.*" He died in 1910. Yes, that was a Halley year.

In ancient times comets were often blamed for floods, earthquakes, disease and destruction. And, Halley's comet welcomed more than a fair share of bad news. Its first appearance in the Common Era took place in the year 66, which was on the eve of the rebellion and eventual destruction of the Jewish temple by the Romans, memorialized in a drawing of Halley's comet over the city of Jerusalem. The list of momentous (sad) historical events continues through the ages, including its appearance in 1759—the year of Halley's vindication—corresponding with the Conquest of Canada.

The next appearance of Halley's comet—technically the perihelion, when it comes closest to the sun—is scheduled for July 28, 2061. On that particular date I hope to be retired, approaching 95 and in good health—trying to beat the Gompertz odds—and enjoying my wife, kids and grandkids while living off my university pension, which, according to Halley, is quite valuable. And, unlike Mark Twain, I hope not to go out with the comet.

CHAPTER 4

WHAT IS A PROPER SPENDING RATE?

EQUATION #4: IRVING FISHER (1867–1947)

$$\ln[c_{x+1}] - \ln[c_x] = \frac{r - \rho + \ln[p_x]}{\gamma}$$

A t this point in the narrative, I hope that conversations about retirement income planning will be based on the following three principles. First, as Benjamin Gompertz pointed out, the amount of *time* you will spend in retirement is random. Planning for averages is plain sloppy, because you face longevity risk either way. Second, Leonardo Fibonacci taught us the strict mathematical relationship between the amount of money you plan to *spend* each year of retirement and the amount of *time* the money will actually last. Third and finally, a government or corporate pension annuity, or private annuity that you can purchase from an insurance company, which pays income for the rest of your life, is quite valuable. The younger you are when you retire, and the lower the prevailing interest rate in the economy, the more valuable the pension annuity. You should know this from the astronomer Edmond Halley.

Who you have not heard from yet is a *bona fide* economist. In this chapter you will learn about the greatest economic scholar of the first half of the 20th century, Professor Irving Fisher. Some have called him the American John Maynard Keynes (who was British). Irving Fisher's contributions to retirement economics go far beyond the one equation I have chosen to display atop this chapter—the one which I will soon explain—but I'll do my best to give many of his other ideas credit.

Economists had long known how to think about the tradeoff between a bushel of soybeans and a barrel of crude oil, for example. This involved the famous concepts of supply and demand. But at one point in time, Irving Fisher the economist was the first to properly formulate how *rational consumers* should adjust their consumption spending over time. This is the intertemporal aspect of economic tradeoffs. He was the first to tell us how to properly accumulate and spend our nest egg, which is exactly what this chapter's about.

Irving Fisher was born in 1867 and served as a professor of economics at Yale from 1898 to 1935. He was a prolific writer in both academic and popular media. It seems he was the first celebrity economist who was venerated and often quoted by the media of his time. If there had been a CNBC television channel in the 1920s, feeding the speculators and day traders, it is quite likely Fisher would have been a regular guest commentator. He gave thousands of speeches and was a consultant to governments and corporations. Yes, he was hot.

Unfortunately, his credibility and celebrity status came to a thunderous end around the stock market meltdown of 1929. Just before the crash, Professor Fisher announced to the media and world at large that "stock prices are at a permanently high plateau" and he was quite bullish. Talk about bad timing! No one could change his mind, and Fisher continued his optimistic and no-cause-for-worry message as the American economy fell into the Great Depression.

But it wasn't just Fisher's intellectual reputation that took a hit. So did his personal finances. He actually put his money where his mouth was, and lost $10 million—which in today's inflation-adjusted values would be close to $140 million—in the stock market crash of 1929. For the rest of his life, he survived off personal loans from his sister-in-law, loans that he could never pay back.

Now, you may wonder why anyone might take retirement planning advice from someone who crashed so spectacularly. But hopefully I'll convince you of Fisher's contributions to retirement economics—which have recently been rediscovered and appreciated anew—and why they deserve serious consideration. In fact, some have theorized Irving Fisher was right about the stock market all along but that he was about 50 years before his time. You be the judge.

Retirement Inflation: It's Getting Personal

I've emphasized earlier in this book—and will now reiterate that retirement income calculations should be conducted in real (after inflation) terms. This means that all cash flows and interest rates should be expressed in numbers adjusted for inflation. For example, if your nest egg is sitting in a safe bank account earning a meager 1% interest per year but inflation is running at 3% per year then you're effectively earning −2% interest. In other words, your money is not really growing; instead, it's slowly shrinking away. Sure, the balance might appear to get larger each year, but that's an illusion. Its purchasing power is shrinking. Stated differently, the difference between your *nominal* interest rate (1%) and your *real* interest rate (−2%) is the inflation rate, 3%. It's what your money buys that matters.

Irving Fisher was likely the first economist to actually create an *inflation index* by averaging the prices of thousands of goods and services and tracking them over time. He debated many different ways and methodologies for creating these indices and was well aware that if a particular index was biased toward the spending habits of the population as a group, it might not necessarily reflect the experiences of a subgroup such as retirees. In many ways the elderly spend differently and their inflation might be higher.

Thus, it was Irving Fisher who first brought attention to the difference between real and nominal interest rates. In fact, he actually wrote down an equation—not the one in this chapter—relating the two, called Fisher's Inflation equation. He cautioned consumers not to be fooled by nominal rates or inflation illusion, even more reason to pay him tribute in a book on retirement equations—even though my focus in this chapter is spending rates.

Irving Fisher was one of the first to carefully tabulate and create indices of inflation, and was quite vocal in arguing that inflation was a monetary phenomenon. In other words, the reason prices were going up every year was precisely because there was too much money sloshing around the financial system. Today this seems obvious, but at the time most people didn't see the link between the money supply, the quantity of money outstanding and inflation rates. Fisher taught us to focus on returns that are real.

Sustainable Spending Rates: Maybe

If you haven't heard of the infamous *4% rule* of retirement income planning, it's probably for the better. No single number has been more closely associated with retirement planning and no single number has been so widely abused. Let me tell you about the 4% rule and my issues with it.

More than 20 years ago, a well-meaning financial advisor by the name of William Bengen wrote a rather influential article in a trade magazine for financial advisors in which he posed the following question: What is the spending rate that would allow a nest egg to survive exactly 30 years of retirement?

This was a tricky question. If you withdraw too much, your nest egg might be exhausted before the 30 years are over. And if you withdraw too little, you might be left with too much left over at the end of the 30 years of retirement.

William Bengen looked back in time—using decades of stock market data—and determined that if retirees kept their spending to $40,000 per $1 million—or 4%—they'd be okay. If you invested your $1,000,000 in a balanced portfolio of stocks and bonds, and pulled out $40,000 per year adjusted for inflation, it would last for 30 years. So said history. At the end of the 30 years you'd be left with zero on average.

Why 30 years was used or why someone might insist on a constant dollar amount, or why someone might have a balanced—60% stocks and 40% bonds—portfolio was never really addressed in the article. Nor was there any discussion of the problem about whether the past was a proper model for the future. It was a statement of fact. Had someone retired any time between 1926 and 1994 with $1 million and spent $40,000 each year, it would have lasted for 30 years.

At the time the article was published with little notice in a rather obscure journal aimed at financial advisors, but its influence—for better or worse—has been immense. Indeed, almost 20 years after his 1994 article entitled "Determining Withdrawal Rates Using Historical Data" was published, this 4% rule has taken on the status of a mythical beast in the retirement planning world. (You slay it, or it slays you.) The 4% rule implies you need 25 times your desired income as a nest egg at retirement. The 4% rule means you shouldn't spend any more or less. Stick to the 4% rule and you should be fine. It's hard to overestimate or exaggerate how influential the 4% rule has become. Most financial services companies in the retirement business advocate some version of this rule on their websites and in their marketing material. Just Google the phrase "4% rule" and you'll see how central it has become.

Most economists, however, do not take kindly to this rule—I'll explain why soon—and the source of their discomfort can be traced directly to Irving Fisher's ideas about *lifecycle consumption smoothing*. By "smoothing" I mean that you should carefully spread your economic resources over your entire life, as opposed to arbitrarily targeting a particular level or number.

In fact, I believe if Irving Fisher were alive today he'd be appalled at the 4% rule and would be on TV railing against it. Fisher's philosophy was that there was no universal spending or consumption rate and that everyone should pick a number that would best smooth their consumption. It does not have to be fixed or flat over time, and really depends on your personal preferences and especially your attitude toward longevity risk. I'll get to that in a moment.

Figure 4.1 Retirement Expenditures by Aging Population: 50 to 80 (Scaled by Age 50 Value)

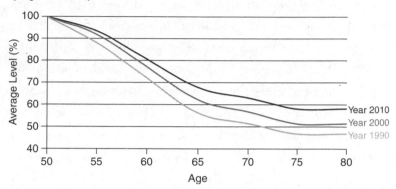

Data Source: U.S. Department of Labor, Bureau of Labor Statistics: http://www.bls.gov/cex/#tables.

Figure 4.1 displays some actual data on retirement expenditure (i.e., cash spending) rates for retirees at various ages, in the years 1990, 2000 and 2010. I've used U.S. numbers (in Fisher's honor), but the exact same pattern can be observed with Canadian, European or even Japanese retirees. It's important to distinguish between expenditures (cash outlays) and the fuzzier and harder to measure consumption, which includes the value of the time you spend performing various activities, such as preparing a seven-course meal.

One thing's certain: notice how the overall expenditure rates start to decline around age 50. By 65, retirees are spending between 50% and 70% of what they did at 50. And, by 80 it has dropped to under 60%. Notice also how the number (and the curve) has increased since the year 1990. People spend relatively *less* in their retirement years compared to when they are 50, but the relatively less has been diminishing over time.

This leads us directly to Equation #4.

The Fourth Equation, Explained

Fisher's equation, Equation #4, is slightly different from the first three equations presented so far. Recall Fibonacci made a prediction, Gompertz offered a forecast and Halley estimated what something is worth. All three equations had no preconceptions about *your preferences or your tastes* other than easily observable quantities. Equation #4, in contrast, is actually telling you what to do. Fisher's suggesting how to behave, offering a blueprint for spending during your retirement years—which, by the way, is consistent with his professorial personality. (More on this later.)

Fisher's equation is written in terms of the difference or change in your consumption rate over one year of retirement, from any age (x) to age ($x+1$). The left-hand side is an approximation for the rate of change (of the natural logarithm) of your consumption rate, which is the change over a very short period of time. Either way, the left-hand side will be zero when there's no change in your consumption rate over time. (Remember, Fisher's telling you how to behave.) The left-hand side is an instruction template for changing your consumption, as he suggests, over time.

The right-hand side of Equation #4 contains the components that effect the change in your consumption rate. There are four variables that should affect your changing consumption rate. They are:

1. The real (after inflation) interest rate your nest egg is earning while it waits to be spent, denoted by (r);

2. Your subjective discount rate, a.k.a. your personal rate of patience, which I'll explain later, denoted by Greek letter rho (ρ);

3. The (natural logarithm of the) probability of surviving for one year, a concept which you should be familiar with from chapters

two and three, written as $ln[p_x]$. The subscript should remind you it is a probability for one year, starting from the age of x. Think of age $x = 60$, or $x = 65$ or $x = 75$.

4. Your risk aversion, and specifically your attitude to longevity uncertainty. The higher the value, the *less chance* you're willing to risk you'll live longer than expected, denoted by (γ).

I know all these letters can get confusing, but I'm just adhering to conventional notation here. Allow me to elaborate.

The first variable in the equation, the interest rate, should be self-explanatory by now. It is the same interest rate used in the Fibonacci and Halley equations. It is the rate—after inflation, of course—at which your money grows over time. (Sometimes we use I for period interest rates, and sometimes we use R for annual interest rates, but it is the same concept.) The second variable, the subjective discount rate, is just a fancy term for how much interest you would *demand* to give up your consumption for a year. The rate you would demand hypothetically isn't necessarily the rate you would receive from the market. Think of (ρ) as the exact opposite of a market interest rate, denoted by (r). The latter number is the best you can get for delaying gratification, and the former is what you would ideally demand to delay gratification. The two numbers should be pretty close to each other in a well-functioning capital market (and household). Many economists theorize that for most people the two are equal (so $\rho = r$), but I personally doubt that applies to everyone.

Here's another completely different way to think about this new concept, your subjective discount rate, rho (ρ).

If you use your high-interest credit card (for luxury and non-essential consumption items) and do not pay off the balance at the end of each month—i.e., paying 18% interest to the banks when they're paying 2% on deposits—then you're revealing you value today's consumption over next year's consumption at the same rate of 18%. Your subjective discount rate is 18% (and Irving Fisher would berate you, by the way).

The key to understanding subjective or personal discount rates is that all you care about is *when* you get the money. Time is all that matters. In other words, the utility value (happiness, bliss) from the $100,000 salary you might receive 10 years from now doesn't depend on whether you made $50,000 or $150,000 the year before. A steep assumption to some—and recently questioned by many behavioral economists—but stay with me. Remember, I'm not trying to explain consumer behavior (i.e., *positive* economics), but to offer some reasonable guidance (i.e., *normative* economics).

Now let's move to the remaining two variables on the right-hand side of Equation #4. The survival probability is always less than one, so its natural logarithm will always be less than zero, or negative. So the lower the survival probability ($ln[_1p_x]$), the higher the probability of dying, and the faster your consumption rate should decline. Remember, ($ln[_1p_x]$) is a negative number. Think about that one for a while and it will make sense, eventually.

Finally, the last and most critical variable on the right-hand side of Fisher's equation is the so-called *longevity risk aversion* (sometimes abbreviated LoRA), and denoted by the letter gamma (γ). This is one of the trickiest numbers in economics, yet central to most of what economists do. According to (classical) economists, every person is endowed with a personal attitude toward risk. Some people hate risk and are unwilling to take a chance, even to obtain possible rewards. Others love risk, and embrace it. I'm sure you know people who fall in either camp. The race car drivers, the gamblers, the skydivers and thrill-seekers exhibit low levels of risk aversion. Think of them as having low gamma (γ) values. At the other extreme are those who are afraid of their own shadow. The conservative investor who parks his/her money in the safest banks and only crosses the street at the crosswalk. You get the point. They have high gamma values.

A more nuanced (modern) view is that people's attitudes toward risk are more malleable, ill-defined and can often be influenced by the context in which the risk is framed. But, everyone has a risk attitude.

Now, Equation #4 itself wasn't quite written that way by Irving Fisher himself. He said this in words in his classic 1930 book called *The Theory of Interest: As Determined by Impatience to Spend Income and Opportunity to Invest It.* Actually, the person responsible for converting Fisher's insight into mathematics was another professor of economics, Menahem Yaari, in a widely cited article he wrote— coincidentally also at Yale—back in 1965.

So here is Fisher's insight in words. There's a very small chance you will spend 30 years in retirement and live to the age of 95. This also means that most retirees will never live to enjoy and appreciate that age. Personally, I'm unwilling to starve myself for the first 30 years of my retirement, on the off chance I make it to 95. I'll reduce my standard of living if I ever reach that age and would rather enjoy a higher standard of living earlier in retirement. In the language of Equation #4, I am not longevity risk averse. My (γ) value is quite low.)

Others—perhaps even you—might think differently. Others might worry about living to 95 and be unwilling to reduce their standard of living if that happens. They must spend less today—and by quite a bit, as you'll soon see—to build up a large enough reserve to last until they reach 95.

Neither of us disagrees about the probability of living to 95—we both agree it's about 10%—but we react to those probabilities differently. You are more longevity risk averse. I am more longevity risk tolerant. This is no different than investing in the stock market, which can be quite risky. You might hate the risk and keep your money in cash. I am less averse to this risk and keep the money in equities.

Fisher's Optimal Retirement Plan, Applied

As promised, here's a detailed example of how to apply Equation #4 with some actual numbers. Start by assuming you're nearing retirement with a nest egg worth approximately $500,000 and you are entitled to a pension annuity paying $25,000 per year, adjusted for inflation. I use the phrase pension annuity in its broadest sense to include both government Social Security (definitely adjusted for inflation) as well as any private annuity income (which may not be). Notice that in this case the ratio of your nest egg to your annual pension income is 20 to 1, which is a nice margin of safety and should allow you to enjoy your nest egg with more confidence—and earlier—compared to someone who might only have a nest egg that is five or eight times their pension income.

The question that Fisher's equation, Equation #4, helps you address is how you should spend down the nest egg as you age, in a way that trades off Gompertz's declining survival probabilities and Fisher's intertemporal choice. To keep things simple, let's further assume your subjective discount rate (think patience) in the absence of longevity risk is equal to the prevailing market interest rate, which I take to be exactly 3%. This is quite a number of assumptions and suppositions, but my point is to help you develop the intuition behind Fisher's equation in the simplest possible environment. What I'm saying is, were it not for longevity risk—i.e., the uncertainty about how long you will live—your preference would be for a flat (non-increasing and non-decreasing) consumption profile over time.

Table 4.1a puts this all together and essentially tells you how to consume in retirement, depending on how much of a chance you're willing to take that you will live longer than you expect. For example, if your longevity risk *aversion* (LoRA) is high, you should start by consuming $51,697 at age 65. Note that $25,000 of this will be your pension income, and the remaining $26,697 should be withdrawn from your $500,000 nest egg. Also note that if you withdraw $26,697 from a portfolio worth $500,000 you are spending approximately 5.34% in your first year of retirement. Contrast this with the conventional wisdom—which I mentioned earlier—of approximately 4%. The reason it is higher than what you might see recommended in the media is twofold. First, the calculations in Table 4.1a assume your money is growing at 3% inflation adjusted per year without any risk, and second, you have a solid pension covering almost half your expenses in your first year of retirement. Table 4.1b does the same for a lower interest rate of 1% per year, and you can see that the consumption numbers across the board are lower.

Notice that in the case of high longevity risk aversion in Table 4.1a, if you happen to still be alive at 100 (which has a 2.4% chance according to Gompertz's law of mortality, Equation #2) you'll be consuming $32,428: a pension of $25,000 and nest-egg withdrawals of $7,428.

Table 4.1a How Should You Rationally Adjust Your Retirement Consumption over Time?

Real Interest Rate = 3%	LOW (1) Longevity Risk Aversion $	MEDIUM (3) Longevity Risk Aversion $	HIGH (8) Longevity Risk Aversion $	Survival Probability %
Age 65	69,426	57,693	51,697	100
Age 66	68,689	57,489	51,628	98.9
Age 70	64,954	56,427	51,269	93.6
Age 80	47,954	50,998	49,360	69.1
Age 90	25,000	38,166	44,276	29.0
Age 95	25,000	28,037	39,441	11.5
Age 100	25,000	25,000	32,428	2.4

Data Source: Calculations by The QWeMA Group.
Mortality rates based on the Gompertz law of mortality.

Now contrast these numbers (high longevity risk aversion) with the values for optimal consumption when longevity risk aversion is low. In this case, the first year's consumption is a much higher $69,426 value, nearly $18,000 more than for the individual with high levels of longevity risk aversion. Now why is this person entitled to enjoy a much higher standard of living early on in retirement? What does she or he know—or what's she or he doing—that entitles her or him to such leisure? The answer, of course, is that there's no secret formula for investment success since they're all earning 3% on their money in Table 4.1a. The key is that those with low levels of longevity risk aversion are willing to take a chance that they have to reduce their standard of living quite dramatically later on *if they happen to still be alive*. Notice that if he's alive at 100—which, again, has a 2.4% chance of materializing—he'll be spending exactly the $25,000 provided by the pension. His nest egg will be completely exhausted and he'll have run out of money.

Table 4.1b How Should You Rationally Adjust Your Retirement Consumption over Time?

Real Interest Rate = 1%	LOW (1) Longevity Risk Aversion $	MEDIUM (3) Longevity Risk Aversion $	HIGH (8) Longevity Risk Aversion $	Survival Probability %
Age 65	64,082	52,219	46,074	100
Age 66	63,402	52,034	46,013	98.9
Age 70	59,954	51,073	45,692	93.6
Age 80	44,262	46,159	43,992	69.1
Age 90	25,000	34,545	39,461	29.0
Age 95	25,000	25,377	35,151	11.5
Age 100	25,000	25,000	28,901	2.4

Data Source: Calculations by The QWeMA Group.
Mortality rates based on the Gompertz law of mortality.

Are you willing to take this chance? Irving Fisher taught the economics profession there's nothing wrong, evil or misguided about spending more early in retirement and less later in retirement. It's a matter of preference and you have to decide what suits you and your preference for risk. But one thing is sure: there's absolutely no reason why your planned consumption must be flat for the rest of your life. Sure, you can do that if you want, but that means you're depriving yourself early on in retirement.

Personally, I suggest that if you're worried about living to 100 with no money, wandering the streets panhandling and in search of soup kitchens (i.e., the bag lady syndrome), get yourself a pension annuity!

In Fisher's Words

Here is what Fisher said in his 1930 classic, which still resonates today:

The uncertainty of life itself casts a shadow on every business transaction into which time enters. Uncertainty of human life increases the rate of preference for present over future income for many people . . . (page 216) Then, when he gets a little older, if his children are married and have gone out into the world and are well able to take care of themselves, he may again have a high degree of impatience for income, because he expects to die, and he thinks: Instead of piling up for the remote future, why shouldn't I enjoy myself during the few years that remain? (page 90)

According to Fisher, picking a constant spending rate number— say, $50,000 per year forever—and sticking to it (come hell or high water) makes no sense. You must adjust to the evolving level of your wealth, and should probably enjoy it all while you can.

Confirming the Numbers

I still owe you one final item: confirmation that the numbers in Table 4.1a and Table 4.1b are in fact consistent with Equation #4. For readers who trust me implicitly or don't care much for proofs, feel free to skip ahead to the next section. For the remainder, here goes.

Take a careful look at Table 4.1b, and specifically the numbers in the third column under the title MEDIUM Longevity Risk Aversion. Notice that at age 65 you plan to consume $52,219, and $52,034 at 66. Now compute the difference between the natural logarithm of both these numbers, roughly 10.85965 minus 10.86320 = −0.00355, or in percentage terms −0.355%, one-third of a percent. This is the left-hand side of Equation #4. Remember this number.

Now let's examine the right-hand side of the equation. You subtract the subjective discount rate (i.e., patience rate) denoted by the Greek letter ρ plus the natural logarithm of the survival probability from the interest rate r. Then you divide by the longevity risk aversion, denoted by γ. In the case of Table 4.1a, the interest rate of 3% was set equal to the subjective discount rate; the only part that matters is the survival probability.

The survival rate for one year is 98.94%. The natural logarithm of this number is −0.0106, approximately −1.1%. Finally, divide by the assumed ($\gamma = 3$) and you're left with −0.355%. *Voilà*. The left- and right-hand sides match.

Do the same for high and low values of longevity risk aversion—then subtract the difference in consumption—and you will roughly get the −1.1% divided by said risk aversion. For example, with high risk aversion the difference in consumption was −0.132% and under low risk aversion the difference was −1.067%. This is exactly the natural logarithm of the survival probability divided by 8 and 1, respectively. Hopefully you are convinced that the numbers in the table obey Fisher's rules.

Irving Fisher's Rise, Fall and Rise Again

Irving Fisher was born in Saugerties, in the upstate New York area called the Catskills, on February 27, 1867. His early family life was quite modest and financially sparse. His father was a pastor at a congressional church, so Irving grew up on regular doses of God, the Bible, Christianity and preaching. Although he didn't enter or desire the ministry, preaching was in his blood.

Among the many personal tragedies in Irving's life was his father's death in 1884, when Irving was merely 17. This forced him into the family breadwinner role, which he maintained—supporting his mother and siblings—by tutoring mathematics while studying at Yale.

Fisher was the epitome of the Yale man of the late 19th century. He completed his undergraduate work there in 1888, graduating first class as a member of the infamous Skull and Bones Society, then completed his doctoral dissertation in 1891. His graduate research and scientific outlook were influenced by the Yale physicist Josiah Willard Gibbs, whom you might recognize as the father of modern chemical thermodynamics. A century later Irving Fisher's dissertation, entitled "Mathematical Investigations in the Theory of Value and Price," is still highly acclaimed because it was the first ever to combine rigorous mathematical analysis and economics. In fact, Paul Samuelson, one of the most illustrious economists of the late 20th century who you will learn more about later, called Irving Fisher's dissertation the best he'd seen—period. Fisher's credentials in scholarly economics were impeccable.

In addition to Fisher's writing on optimal consumption and the evils of inflation illusion—two important topics for retirement planning—he also wrote about best practices in the banking industry. In particular, he was an advocate of a rather unpopular concept called "Narrow Banking." He argued banks should be required to hold 100% reserves against all checking and savings accounts which could be withdrawn at any time. Usually they hold only a fraction of the money under the assumption that it is highly unlikely everyone will want their nest egg (i.e., money) back on the same day. Forcing banks to hold "100% Money" (as Fisher called it) would avoid them going out and speculating (gambling) with the money, and placing the entire financial system at risk. This sort of staunch proposal might resonate to many after the 2008 financial crisis, despite its impracticality. Strands of Irving Fisher's thinking on banking—as well as consumption smoothing—have recently been taken up by another well-known contemporary American economist and 2012 presidential candidate, Laurence Kotlikoff.

Despite being at the center of classical mathematical economics and rational decision making, Fisher also had a soft spot for psychology. Well-known behavioral economist Richard Thaler has argued that Irving Fisher foresaw much of the so-called financial irrationality discoveries of the late 1980s and 1990s—back in the 1920s. Indeed, Fisher's book *The Theory of Interest* made ample use of terms such as self-control, irrationality and personal factors that determine impatience and money illusion. He actually visited Germany during its inflationary periods and interviewed real people, another trademark of behavioral economists.

After getting married in 1893, Fisher traveled widely in Europe, visiting the major universities, and was on a first-name basis with all the (giant) economists of his era. He met with such renowned economists as Francis Ysidro Edgeworth, Alfred Marshall, Carl Menger, Leon Walras, Vilfredo Pareto and Joseph Schumpeter. These are all names—to misquote Floria Tosca—before whom graduate students in economics still tremble. And so, with impeccable connections and impressive publications, Irving Fisher was promoted to full professor of economics at Yale in 1898—the academic base for his entire career.

In 1918, Fisher was elected president of the American Economics Association, the pinnacle of recognition and achievement in his field.

But Irving Fisher had more than economics on his mind. Quite different from most ivory tower academics, he had many other interests and preoccupations far from equations of supply and demand. He was a perennial inventor and entrepreneur. He actually created the first index card system—which you may recall from visiting the library in the days before the Internet—which he subsequently sold for great profit. He also invented and published economic indices, for GDP or inflation, among others, still used today. He pioneered the first index-linked bond which paid coupons in real (as opposed to nominal) terms. Fisher was someone who applied—not just theorized about—his research.

In the public arena, he was a proponent and tireless advocate for the League of Nations, precursor to the United Nations. He was also an outspoken supporter and defender of the 18th amendment to the U.S. Constitution, ultimately ratified by the U.S. Congress in 1919. For readers too young to remember, this introduced Prohibition (a ban on alcohol manufacture and sales) to the land. Irving Fisher was one of its most enthusiastic defenders in books, articles and speeches, which is completely uncharacteristic for an academic economist, most of whom head straight for the bars once a day full of equation manipulation is over.

He was also a board member and spokesperson for the so-called Life Extension Institute, and in that capacity co-wrote a book on hygiene and healthy living. It seems he had an obsession with health and healthy living that could be traced to his battle with tuberculosis in his early 30s. He had to take leave from teaching at Yale and went to a sanatorium for almost three years. Fisher's biographer, Robert Allen, claims in his 1993 book that Fisher returned to active life a changed man. He spent the rest of his life concerned with two things: economic stability and reducing mortality rates. While Fisher told economists how time, aging and mortality uncertainty might affect consumption patterns today, he also did his best to reduce population mortality rates.

In fact, Fisher's health-related book sold millions of copies and became a bestseller. The book, co-written with Dr. Eugene Lyman Fisk, was called *How to Live: Rules for Healthful Living Based on Modern Science*, and went through various editions. It contained admonishments on the consumption of alcohol, tobacco, salt, pepper, condiments, coffee, tea and sugar in concentrated form. No coffee? No alcohol? Jeez. Irving Fisher was quite the humorless fellow.

Some nuggets in his book on hygiene, such as warnings about weight, were ahead of their time and quite reasonable: "Life insurance experience has clearly shown that weight, especially in relation to age, is an important factor in influencing longevity" (Fisher and Fisk, page 30).

The more esoteric and humorous ones included:

> There is an unreasonable prejudice against air in motion. A gentle draft is, as a matter of fact, one of the best friends which the seeker after health can have. Of course, a strong draft directed against some exposed part of the body, causing a local chill for a prolonged time, is not desirable. (Fisher and Fisk, page 8)

And here's one of my personal favorites:

> At times we can enjoy relief from clothing altogether. Anyone can spend a little time in a state of nature . . . there are many things which are usually done while one's clothes are on which could be done just as well while they are off. Brushing the teeth, washing the hands, shaving. (Fisher and Fisk, page 16)

Laugh all you want. This book was published in 1915, had a foreword written by none other than William H. Taft, president of the United States from 1909 to 1913, then sold millions of copies and underwent more than 90 reprints. The book made Fisher a household name in the United States, not to mention the nice fortune in royalties he was able to collect from book sales, and additional recognition through speeches and spinoff articles.

Some other nuggets from his bestseller were less amusing. His involvement in the eugenics movement, which advocated improving a population's genetic composition by proper breeding, helps shed light on Fisher, the person. Here's a direct quote from the same book on hygiene:

> In the light of modern eugenics we could make a new human race in a hundred years if only people in positions of power and influence would wake up to the paramount importance of what Eugenics means . . . It could be done by segregation of the sexes for defectives, feeble-minded idiots, epileptics, insane, etc. By this kind of isolation we can save the blood stream of our race from a tremendous amount of needless contamination. (Fisher and Fisk, page 322)

Yes, Irving Fisher had a darker side.

The 1929 Crash

Irving Fisher is most widely known for his terribly misguided optimism about the stock market and the economy before and during the Great Depression. This wasn't the case of a comment taken out of context or a minor quote that came back to haunt him. He really got it spectacularly wrong.

In early September 1929, the U.S. stock market reached a record high, and some public commentators started worrying prices were exhibiting what we might call "bubble tendencies" today. But Fisher would have none of it. He gave an interview to the *New York Times* in which he forcefully discredited the naysayers. Nonsense, he said, taking the opportunity to buy more stocks. He was bullish and his portfolio was heavily leveraged with margin debt and bank loans.

On October 14, 1929, he gave a major speech, excerpted by the media, in which he claimed the "stock market would be much higher" in just a few months. On Monday, October 21, 1929, he gave a presentation to a large audience of credit analysts in New York City reaffirming his optimism. He gave another speech to a group of bankers on Wednesday, October 23, using phrases like "new economic era" (sound familiar?) and "new high plateau."

Then, on October 24, 1929 (a.k.a. Black Thursday), the stock market crashed, erasing years of spectacular growth. Bank failures ensued and the period known as the Great Depression began unfolding. It would be another four years before stock markets actually hit bottom. Fisher was ruined. He never quite came to grips with what happened, either intellectually or financially. To make matters worse, Fisher ended up enduring financial troubles which included years of battles with the U.S. Internal Revenue Service (IRS) over taxes they claimed he owed on profits he'd made in the run-up to the stock market crash. Talk about adding insult to injury.

Although Irving Fisher has much to teach us about retirement income planning, his own retirement didn't quite work out as planned. During his golden years, when most retirees are slowly drawing down their nest egg, Fisher's balance sheet had a negative net worth since he owed millions of dollars to a variety of lenders. Sadly, he had to sell his beloved home near Yale because he couldn't afford the payments. He spent his last years living under financial stress and juggling his debts—but proud, defiant and overly optimistic to the end.

IRVING FISHER (1867–1947)

It's quite remarkable how Irving Fisher, who contributed so much to our understanding and language of rational economic tradeoffs, consumption smoothing, balance-sheet risk management, inflation awareness and general planning for the long run, failed so miserably in his own financial planning.

Indeed, though he didn't leave much of a financial legacy, Fisher left a monumental economic legacy—one that's still very much appreciated a century later.

CHAPTER 5

HOW MUCH IN RISKY STOCKS VERSUS SAFE CASH?

EQUATION #5: PAUL SAMUELSON (1915–2009)

$$\psi = \frac{1}{\gamma}(HC + FC)\left(\frac{\mu - r}{\sigma^2}\right)$$

In March of 1997, MIT Professor Paul Samuelson, the Nobel Prize-winning economist, wrote a scathing letter to an impetuous and newly minted Ph.D.—a few days shy of his 30th birthday—to tell him his most recent scholarly paper was misguided and erroneous. Professor Samuelson's main concern was that the author of the paper—a paper that was about to be published in a scholarly journal—was implicitly advocating excessive investment in risky stocks under the premise that the odds of losing money declined with time.

Professor Samuelson claimed the declining probabilities in and of themselves were irrelevant and that their small magnitude must be balanced by Fisher's "disutilities of loss."

In plain English, if there was a mere 1% chance of losing 25% of your nest egg in the stock market, and that chance caused you sufficient psychic pain, the stock market should be avoided. There's a 1-in-10,000 chance your house burns down, yet you buy fire insurance. Odds are only one part of a proper economic story.

The wet-behind-the-ears assistant professor of finance who got the unexpected scolding from the greatest economic scholar of the late 20th century was none other than yours truly, and this chapter is my chance for penance.

Time Is on Your Side?

The mid-to-late 1990s was the worst possible time for many graduate students in economics and finance (like me) specializing in the stock market. The Dow Jones Industrial Average (DJIA), the most visible measure of broad market performance, first closed above the 4,000 level in February 1995. The DJIA hit the 5,000 level in November 1995, then 6,000 in October 1996, 7,000 in February 1997, 8,000 in July 1997, 9,000 in April 1998 and finally 10,000 in March 1999. What this means is that during a period of five years the typical stock portfolio had doubled in value and during a decade it had almost tripled. Unprecedented—and so far unrepeated.

The reason this historical run-up was actually quite bad for young researchers is twofold, in my opinion. First, as starving graduate students we really had no money to invest in the bubbly stock market and ended up watching this excitement from the intellectual sidelines. Few of us could borrow or leverage ourselves—who exactly would lend us the money? And those of us who could access a line of credit or buy on margin were wary of what had happened to Irving Fisher in 1929. In the language of economics, although we had plenty of *human capital*—the measure of future potential—we had no *financial capital*. Moreover, Merrill Lynch and Morgan Stanley stockbrokers wouldn't accept my human capital for margin calls.

The second, and more significant, reason why this period wasn't generous to young researchers is that many of us formed unrealistic expectations and beliefs about the stock market. Our theorizing was colored by our immediate experience. We thought it was normal for markets to go up 20% or 30% per year. Yes, it puzzled us—and was fodder for many research papers trying to explain this *fact*—but we experienced bull markets year after year, during a formative period of our intellectual development.

Sure, we witnessed periodic episodes of volatility and market fluctuations. But inevitably markets bounced back a few months later. Even the famed stock market crash of October 1987, which wiped out 25% of stock market value in one day—which many of us did remember—quickly reversed itself a few months later. Two years after the 1987 crash, it was all but erased from investors' personal balance sheets. (Not so the distant crash of 1929, which took decades to undo.)

In the language of psychologists and behavioral economists, our research suffered from a "recency effect." To put it bluntly, the investment and asset allocation models we built during that period were wildly optimistic. I am embarrassed today to reread old books and articles of mine in which I assumed stocks could be expected to earn 15% per year. (Sadly, these words are immortalized in books still available for sale on eBay and Amazon, so I can't shred them all!)

Yes, there were some prescient warnings by well-regarded academics, most notably by academic economists Rajnish Mehra and Edward Prescott, or Robert Shiller more publicly, that stock market returns were too good to be true and couldn't be explained within conventional models. But many younger researchers and especially eager practitioners assumed that *time was on their side.* It seemed all you needed was a few years in the stock market and your money would double or triple. Any dips were to be used as buying opportunities. Mutual fund companies advertised loudly on bus stops, coffee shops and highway billboards: *buy, hold and prosper.*

At some level, time does tell a corroborating tale. Figure 5.1 displays a graph of the famous Dow Jones Industrial Average (DJIA) during the last 100 years. If you cover the right-most side of the picture, then from the perspective of the late-1990s and looking back over a century, it looked like the stock market was the only place to be. The crash of 1929 and even 1987 are minor blips on the chart.

Equity advocates and promoters went so far as to argue that, despite the daily ups and downs, stocks were actually *safe* in the long run. Some readers might have heard of Professor Jeremy Siegel's bestselling 1994 book, *Stocks for the Long Run*, which made the same case. In fact, Professor Siegel was a regular guest on CNBC and other financial talk shows, actively promoting stock investing. Young graduate students such as me could only watch in awe.

Figure 5.1 A Century of the Dow Jones Industrial Average (DJIA)

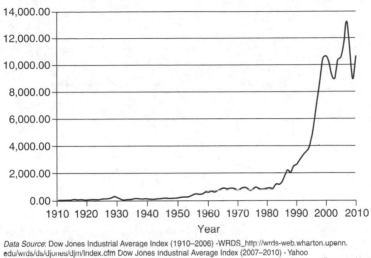

Data Source: Dow Jones Industrial Average Index (1910–2006) -WRDS_http://wrds-web.wharton.upenn.
edu/wrds/ds/djones/djm/index.cfm Dow Jones Industrial Average Index (2007–2010) - Yahoo

Computed by:
Minjie Zhang, Fall 2011

Figure 5.2 provides another perspective on the same long-term phenomenon, and should be reminiscent of Figures 2.1a and 2.1b in Chapter Two for mortality rates. Instead of the *probability of dying* in a given year, the figure uses data for the level of the Standard & Poor's 500 index, then computes the natural logarithm. Notice how the numbers fall relatively close to the trend line, but the fit isn't as good as the one for mortality rates. (It just goes to show you biological laws are more reliable than economic laws.) There are decades in which the market was under the trend line, and decades in which they were above the trend line. The point of this chart, of course, is to illustrate that over the previous century—just like over your natural life, for mortality rates—these numbers increase steadily. This, yet again, has been taken as evidence for the superiority of stocks in the long run.

Figure 5.2 Natural Logarithm of Inflation-adjusted SP500 Index

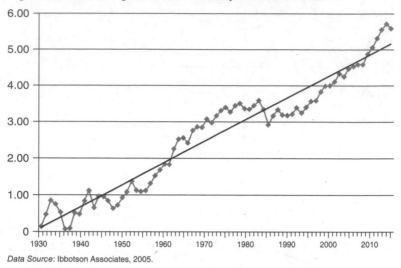

Data Source: Ibbotson Associates, 2005.

From a purely mathematical point of view, the "stocks are safer over long periods of time" argument—before Samuelson took an ax to it—went as follows.

Historically, there was a 35% chance a diversified portfolio (such as the SP500 Index) of stocks would underperform or earn less than safe cash during any one-year period. So said the data. There was a 65% chance you win, and a 35% chance you don't. The losing side of the equity bet was called the annualized *probability of shortfall*. Moreover, the stock market's behavior from year to year exhibited the same independence as consecutive coin tosses: the coin has no memory of its past behavior and neither, so it was believed, does the stock market. Finally, put these two assumptions together and you get the following: over a two-year period there's a $(0.35)(0.35) = 12.25\%$ probability of shortfall (i.e., losing money). Over a three-year period there is a

$(0.35)(0.35)(0.35) = 4.3\%$ probability of shortfall, etc. Continuing this logic, by year 10 there was a 1-in-40,000 chance you would regret investing in a portfolio of stocks versus safe cash. This mathematically contrived justification was labeled *time diversification* and became another rallying cry of the "buy, hold and prosper" crowd. A longer time period, it was believed—just like a large enough portfolio—diversified away risk. The stock market was a casino in which the odds were heavily in the gamblers' favor, or so we thought at the time.

Now, let me make absolutely clear: there's nothing wrong or misguided about holding a diversified portfolio of great companies such as Apple, Exxon, Microsoft or Walmart for a year, a decade or longer. In fact, as a non-starving non-graduate student, I now own plenty of them and many more. The challenge is how to measure and explain the risk.

The problem with a pure probability approach—which I outlined above—was that: i) it ignored the *magnitude* of how bad things might get when stocks performed poorly, and ii) it ignored retirement withdrawals, otherwise known as the *sequence-of-returns* (SoR) effect. I'll explain what exactly SoR means in Chapter Seven when I discuss something called a *retirement sustainability analysis* (yes, more jargon). But here's the bottom line: researchers and practitioners didn't quite comprehend how bad things might get in the shortfall years.

Enter Paul Samuelson and many of his disciples—including, notably, Boston University Professor Zvi Bodie during the 1990s bubble—who argued that if an investment was risky over one year, time didn't make it any safer. The only safe asset—they claimed—was a risk-free, inflation-adjusted government bond. Anything else carried risk, and that risk didn't disappear in the long run—or even the very long run. Samuelson argued that time alone was not an excuse to hold more stocks. Time did not diversify away risk. Time was not on your side. In fact, time was irrelevant, he said. Thus, it didn't matter how old or young you were. The fact that the probability of shortfall declined quite rapidly with time didn't imply you should skew your portfolio more heavily toward stocks when you were young versus when you were old.

In his letter to me, and in many scholarly articles he published (some even before I was born), Samuelson argued that a very small shortfall probability was offset by the enormous pain from loss. His great flash of genius was to demonstrate that these two effects *exactly* balanced themselves out. The declining probability of loss multiplied by the increasing disutility of loss canceled each other out under most conditions. Ergo, the optimal amount of stocks versus bonds was time-invariant. In other words, the time variable dropped out of Equation #5, which I'll soon get to in greater detail.

Here's what Samuelson had to say in an article he wrote in 1969:

> Investing for many periods does not itself introduce extra tolerance for riskiness at early, or any, stages of life. . . . Our model denies the validity of the concept of businessman's risk. For isoelastic marginal utilities, in your prime of life you have the same risk-tolerance as toward the end of life! The 'chance to recoup' and the tendency for the law of large numbers to operate in the case of repeated investments is not relevant . . . (pages 240, 245)

Samuelson accepted that the trend line displayed in Figure 5.2 was an accurate representation of how stock market prices evolved over time. But he argued that Figure 5.2 was just one realization of a very long series of coin tosses. History may or may not repeat itself. But there are no guarantees. Risk is ever present.

So, you might wonder, why is the financial industry encouraging people who are saving for retirement to invest more in the stock market and take on more risk? Is there any justification for this advice? And did Paul Samuelson actually own any stocks?

Human Capital: You Are Wealthier than You Think

I mentioned earlier that despite Paul Samuelson's warning about the riskiness of stocks, which I've taken to heart, I personally remain (today) heavily invested in them—for better or worse. The reason I've made this seemingly risky decision is because I am many years away from retirement. In fact, I have a very long time horizon before I plan to stop working at age 70, and start collecting my pension income from the university where I'm employed.

Now, if you've been paying any attention at all, your first reaction might be: "Didn't he read anything he just wrote in the previous paragraph? Doesn't he get it? Professor Samuelson proved that time shouldn't matter."

But the fact is that I actually agree 100% with Samuelson, and my behavior is perfectly consistent with his recommendations. In fact, Samuelson himself would agree because I am using my *entire capital* to determine the risky quotient of my financial capital. This might sound confusing at first, and I promise I'll explain what this all means in a moment. For now, the key to reconciling the above-stated Samuelson *time invariance* (or irrelevance) and the investment advice doled out by industry—and my own behavior—is a concept I briefly alluded to earlier, namely *human capital.*

Now, this is not quite the proper location to delve too deeply into the topic of human capital (and I actually wrote two entire books devoted to this topic a few years ago) but I believe it's one of the key ingredients to a proper asset allocation.

The basic idea behind "human capital" thinking, popularized by economists from Alfred Marshall at Cambridge University in the late 19th century, to Gary Becker at the University of Chicago in the late 20th century, is as follows.

There are two types of assets (or wealth) a person might possess on their personal balance sheet. The first is *financial capital,* which is quite visible and market-based. Think of money in the bank, bonds in a retirement account or stocks in a portfolio. Consider a car you actually own or a house you've paid off, or even an old stamp collection, or a diamond ring or gold watch. You can sell them anytime and immediately consume the proceeds. This is your financial capital.

But you also own another asset, and that is your income-earning ability. This asset is called your *human capital.* The fact you can work and generate income from your labor is clearly an asset of sorts. Think of a small gold mine or an oil well. Each day only a little bit of gold or oil can be extracted and sold—perhaps generating a few thousand dollars of profit per day—but the value of the mine or well can be worth millions of dollars in the open market. This is why mining companies are worth billions of dollars on the stock market. These companies may not have much or any cash, but they have proven reserves and potential. That is what gives them value.

By going to school, college and university you are effectively investing time and money to create more human capital for yourself. Researchers such as Professor Gary Becker have computed how much an extra year of education can impact your earnings profile over your life. Evidently, the rate of return from investing in education is between 8% and 15%, depending on your field and major. Some careers are obviously worth much more than others, and a recent article

(October 2011) in the *Wall Street Journal* indicated that unemployment rates and earnings can differ quite dramatically based on what you studied in college or university.

One thing is certain: the younger you are—and this is key—the more human capital you have. In other words, the more valuable it is. Sure, you don't get a statement from the bank manager or the stockbroker telling you the value of your human capital, but it's worth quite a bit today. In addition to recognizing its importance, you should probably insure and protect it as well.

I will return to the concept of protecting the human life value in Chapter Six, when I discuss another pioneer and hero, Solomon Huebner. For now the important takeaway is: if you define your wealth broadly enough to include both human and financial capital—and your human capital is relatively safe—then even Paul Samuelson will agree that time and age matter, and that youth can be used to justify having money in the stock market. The question is how much, and that's exactly where Equation #5 fits.

The Equation, Explained

Equation #5 contains a number of variables you've seen previously, and two newer ones. Like Irving Fisher's equation, this one also tells you how to behave and what to do, as opposed to being a prediction of the future or the price of an asset.

Here are the six factors or variables that should determine how much money you should (risk and) invest in the stock market. The amount (in dollars) is denoted by the Greek letter psi (ψ) and based on Samuelson's above-referenced research:

1. The amount of financial capital (i.e., money in the bank) you've accumulated already, denoted by the letters FC. This is measured in dollars.

2. The value of your human capital, measured in dollars (as well), and denoted by the letters HC. Make a conservative estimate of what you think you will earn between now and retirement in real after-inflation terms—but net of any income taxes and required expenditures—then compute its present value. For young college graduates, this number could be in the millions.

3. Your expectation of the rate at which you (or the experts) think stocks will grow over time, denoted by the letter mu (μ). Historically this number has been around 7% for stocks, once inflation is accounted for. It's worth noting that this number (μ) is likely the most contentious number in all of financial economics. Hundreds and possibly thousands of research articles have been written in the last half-century, trying to pin down (μ). I would stick close to the historical 7%, although it might be as low as 5% in today's economic environment. For those who are technically inclined, this is the arithmetic (not geometric) mean.

4. Your expectation for the volatility of stocks, denoted by sigma (σ), which has been around 20% for a well-diversified portfolio of stocks. This is a purely objective (statistical) number, best determined by a statistician. Some argue it might be as high as 25% or even 30%. Of course, the equation gives you the freedom to test a variety of values and see the impact on results.

5. The interest rate available from the safest possible investment (r), which I took to be in the 1% to 4% range in previous chapters, and is probably closer to the low-end of the range today. It obviously represents the alternative to the stocks. If you allocate 90% to stocks, you would be allocating 10% to cash, and vice versa. There are multi-investment extensions of Equation #5 to include

additional asset classes and investment categories, but the main idea is the same.

6. Your risk aversion, denoted by (γ), which we took to be in the region of 1 to 8 in the earlier discussion of Irving Fisher. This is a purely psychological value only you can determine. You may not be able to pin a number to it, which is why I'll give you results based on broad ranges. The key here is the philosophical view that everyone has an attitude toward financial risk and that it can be expressed or summarized in a number. Some have greater tolerance, others do not. Your allocation will depend on your tolerance for risk.

Notice that this equation says nothing (explicitly) about age, time horizon, mortality rates, or even if stocks have been doing well recently. Whether you are 20, 50 or 80, Samuelson's asset allocation equation tells you to consider your attitude toward risk, your total wealth and the long-term view of the market—but not the time horizon. It's nowhere to be found in the equation explicitly, but it is there implicitly.

Here's how it all comes together.

Assume you have $500,000 in financial capital (FC) and the estimated value of your human capital (HC) is also $500,000. Recall that human capital is a present value exercise—discovered by Fibonacci—and involves discounting your available cash flows by a suitable interest rate. Assume further that the risk-free rate of interest is 2% and that you expect to earn 8% from stocks, with a volatility of 20%. In this case $\frac{\mu - r}{\sigma^2} = 1.5$ units. Think of this number as a risk/return ratio. The bigger the ratio, the more attractive it is to invest in stocks versus safe cash, all else being exactly equal. Note that this is a very optimistic perspective on stocks versus cash, a perspective that might not be shared by all. Later we can analyze a more pessimistic case.

Multiply the 1.5 by $1 million in total (human + financial) capital and you get that people who exhibit (or feel) risk aversion $\gamma = 1$ should invest $\psi = \$1.5$ million in the stock market. Those who are more risk averse, with $\gamma = 3$, should invest $\psi = \$500,000$ in the stock market. And those with $\gamma = 8$ should invest only $\psi = \$187,500$ in the stock market. So says Samuelson's equation. As a percentage of your $500,000 financial capital, these numbers would be 300% ($\gamma = 1$), 100% ($\gamma = 3$) and 38% ($\gamma = 8$). Remember, the equation's left-hand side is in dollars. You can express the dollar values as a percent of your investable financial capital (FC) by dividing ψ/FC.

So, while more time—or youth—itself is not a justification for taking a bigger chance with your money, if you consider how wealthy you *really* are, a relatively small allocation of your financial capital to stocks might not be as risky as you think.

When you think about it, time is really embedded inside Samuelson's equation, because the human capital value gets smaller, eventually hitting zero, as you age. Once you reach retirement—defined as the date you stop working permanently, when you have no more human capital and all your wealth is tied up in financial capital— perhaps stocks really are too risky for you. You'll have to decide.

The Equation, Applied: Case Studies and Examples

To make sure this is clear, here are a few more numerical examples.

Assume you're relatively young (a decade before retirement) and have financial capital (i.e., actual savings) of only $50,000. You also have a secure job with an income whose present value you estimate at $1 million. For example, you might earn $100,000 per year after tax and essential expenditures and plan to work for another 10 years. Not accounting for the time value of money, this leads to a human capital value of $1 million. As I mentioned earlier, computing this number involves more art than science, but bear with me for the exercise. Let's further assume your outlook on the stock market—or the consensus from economists—is that real inflation-adjusted values will grow by 8% (quite optimistic) with a variability of 20%, when the current risk-free (safest bonds) rate is 2%. In this case the risk/return ratio is the same 1.5 units, described above.

According to Samuelson's equation, Equation #5, as displayed in Table 5.1, you should have a very substantial amount of your financial capital (i.e., portfolio) invested in stocks. If you experience (or exhibit) low levels of risk aversion, then you should invest an (eye-popping) 3,150% of your financial capital in stocks. I know of no exchange-traded fund (ETF) that can expose you to that kind of leverage, so in all likelihood you must take whatever you can get. Even if you experience high levels of risk aversion, according to the equation you should still have about 400% of your financial capital in stocks. In essence, Samuelson's equation is counseling you to borrow three times your $50,000 savings and go all in—if somebody's willing to lend it to you.

Table 5.1 How Much to Stocks? (Optimistic)

Risk-Free Rate: >	2%						
Expected Return: >	8%		LOW Level of Risk Aversion $\gamma=1$		HIGH Level of Risk Aversion $\gamma=8$		
Stock Volatility: →	20%						
Financial Capital (FC) ($)	Human Capital (HC) ($)	Risk/Return Ratio	$ Invested in Stocks	% of FC in Stocks	$ Invested in Stocks	% of FC in Stocks	
50,000	1,000,000	1.5	1,575,000	3,150	196,875	394	
500,000	1,000,000	1.5	2,250,000	450	281,250	56	
1,000,000	1,000,000	1.5	3,000,000	300	375,000	38	
500,000	500,000	1.5	1,500,000	300	187,500	38	
1,000,000	50,000	1.5	1,575,000	158	196,875	20	
1,000,000	500,000	1.5	2,250,000	225	281,250	28	
750,000	0	1.5	1,125,000	150	140,625	19	

What are we to make of the equation's enormous amount of recommended leverage? It seems uncharacteristic of Samuelson's warnings and admonitions about the stock market. Why would his equation recommend so much stock exposure?

The answer, of course, lies in the $1 million in safe human capital that was an input to the equation. What Samuelson and his disciples—most notably Robert Merton and Zvi Bodie—are saying is that *if* you have a very secure job that is almost cash-like in its security, you can afford to take some big risks with your small stake. But the key is job security, and a long projected working career—although not necessarily time.

The flip side is even more important. If you don't trust your human capital—that is, if you have low levels of job security—and/or if the job you have is quite sensitive to the performance of the stock market itself, then you'd use a much smaller number for HC in Samuelson's equation. Naturally, the resulting amount allocated to the stock market would decline as well. Think of someone who works in the financial industry. Their human capital already contains exposure to stocks, and therefore Samuelson's equation—properly used—would advocate a greater allocation to safer cash.

Now, look at what happens in the table when we only allow for (say) $50,000 in human capital and 20 times that amount in financial capital. This would be quite typical for someone a year or two from retirement—with very little remaining human capital—but whose pension nest egg is worth $1 million. In this case, Table 5.1 recommends 158% leverage for the individual with low risk aversion. This might still seem high, but recall that this is much lower than (the insane) 3,150%. More telling is the allocation to stocks for the individual with high levels of risk aversion. In this case Samuelson's

Table 5.2 How Much to Stocks? (Pessimistic)

Risk-free Rate: → 2%
Expected Return: → 4%
Stock Volatility: → 20%

Financial Capital (FC) ($)	Human Capital (HC) ($)	Risk/Return Ratio	LOW Level of Risk Aversion $\gamma = 1$		HIGH Level of Risk Aversion $\gamma = 8$	
			$ Invested in Stocks	% of FC in Stocks	$ Invested in Stocks	% of FC in Stocks
50,000	1,000,000	0.5	525,000	1,050	65,625	131
500,000	1,000,000	0.5	750,000	150	93,750	19
1,000,000	1,000,000	0.5	1,000,000	100	125,000	13
500,000	500,000	0.5	500,000	100	62,500	13
1,000,000	50,000	0.5	525,000	53	65,625	7
1,000,000	500,000	0.5	750,000	75	93,750	9
750,000	0	0.5	375,000	50	46,875	6

equation dictates that only 20% of his $1 million nest egg be in the stock market—which is quite intuitive.

Table 5.2 provides more of the same. It differs from Table 5.1 in one crucial element, namely the magnitude of the expected return from the stock—denoted by the letter (μ). Think bullish versus bearish. In Table 5.1, I assumed (hoped) stocks would earn 8%; in Table 5.2, I assumed they'd earn 4% per year. This is a mere 2% above the risk-free rate. In this case the risk/return ratio between the excess return of stocks above cash ($\mu - r$) and the volatility squared (σ^2) is exactly 0.5, which is displayed in the third column. The 0.5 value is lower than the 1.5 in Table 5.1. In plain English: I assume stocks don't look as attractive. And so, under a more pessimistic outlook on stocks, the optimal allocations are markedly lower. The direction should be rather obvious. Notice that someone who has equal amounts of financial capital and human capital—half a million or a million of each—would allocate 13% of their financial capital to stocks under high levels of risk aversion.

Notice that when you have $750,000 in financial capital (your nest egg) and no more human capital (you are completely retired) the optimal amount of the nest egg that should be in stocks is a mere 6%, assuming you are highly risk averse. This means that almost your entire nest egg should be sitting in cash, even though you have two or three more decades to live and time is on your side. But, as Samuelson said, time doesn't matter. It's what you're doing with your time that counts. If you are no longer working, have no more human capital and are spending down capital, one can make an argument for absolutely no equity or stocks at all. It all comes down to your risk aversion.

In sum, here's what Samuelson's equation, Equation #5, is *not* saying. Just because you have a long time to go before you plan to retire, or you have a long time to live according to Benjamin Gompertz, it is not an excuse to increase your exposure to stocks in your portfolio. It also depends on the composition of your personal balance sheet, the amount of human versus financial capital and—most importantly—your attitude to financial risk.

Paul Samuelson was quite open to the possibility that if people's preference or attitude toward financial risk fluctuates as they get older or wealthier, they might naturally change their asset allocation as a function of time. But he made it quite clear it wasn't time itself that was inducing the change, but other factors.

In his letter to me, he had the following to say:

> I do not favor or disfavor any changes in equity tolerance induced by lengthening of the investment horizon. What I argue is that a risk-averse person who is an expected utility of wealth maximizer, will not by any valid application of the law of large numbers have to be more equity tolerant when time is large. For some functions she will become less equity tolerant and for some others more tolerant. (Samuelson, 1997)

As his obituary in the *New York Times* noted, Paul Samuelson preached and practiced humility. His final words in his letter to me were: "Take my cold water with many grains of salt. As Max Planck said, science progresses funeral by funeral." Needless to say, that letter is framed on my office wall.

Retirees Should Protect Their Equities

At this point you might be wondering: "Okay, I am approaching my retirement years. Should I get out of the stock market? Sure, Equation #5 tells me how much of my financial capital I should have in the stock market, but based on assumed input values Table 5.1 and Table 5.2 seem to justify a wide range. What to do?"

Well, here are some tips and insights based on Samuelson's equation:

1. Although you'll probably spend two to three decades in retirement and the *odds look good* for equity, if you are risk averse don't let the favorable probabilities distract you from your fears. Although there might be only a 35% chance that stocks earn less than the cash in your low-yielding bank account, if something goes wrong early in retirement—as you're withdrawing money to live off—you might not be able to recover.

2. If you are still working and have the flexibility to delay your retirement by a few years, you can afford to create more human capital if needed. By having the option to create more human capital, you are wealthier than you think and you can afford to take on more risk. This can actually be attributed to the insights of Robert Merton, Zvi Bodie and William Samuelson (Paul's son) in a highly influential paper published in the early 1990s.

3. Paul Samuelson's equation, Equation #5, teaches us that volatility—as measured by the Greek letter (σ)—is a key determinant

of your optimal exposure and allocation to stocks. Recall that it affected the risk/return ratio in Table 5.1 and Table 5.2. Anything you can do, therefore, to reduce the fluctuation or volatility of your portfolio without dramatically reducing your portfolio's investment return (μ) is welcome. For example, "structured equity products" and other "protected equity investments"—broad terms covering many strategies and products that reduce downside risk—have an important role to play in the optimal retirement portfolio. I believe these will grow in popularity and usage as more baby boomers retire.

Paul Samuelson's Life and Impact

Paul A. Samuelson—who passed away at 94, just a few years ago in December 2009—had much in common with the four other protagonists we've seen thus far. Like Leonardo Fibonacci, he wrote a very successful book that made him rich and famous. His college textbook, modestly called *Economics*, was first published in 1948. It has been translated into 20 languages, is now in its 18th edition and has been used by millions of undergraduates for more than 60 years. Like Irving Fisher, Samuelson was a prolific professor of economics who spent most of his academic life at one university, namely MIT. While Irving Fisher was on a first-name basis with presidents William Taft and Franklin Roosevelt, Paul Samuelson served as a private tutor and academic advisor to President John F. Kennedy in the early 1960s. Paul Samuelson lost his father at the age of 23, while Irving Fisher lost his at 18. Both claimed this early loss dramatically impacted their careers. The early death of a parent was also experienced by Edmond Halley; recall that his father was likely murdered.

Unlike Irving Fisher, Paul Samuelson didn't lose his fortune in a stock market crash and was quite aware—and reminded others—of the riskiness of the stock market. Like Benjamin Gompertz, Paul Samuelson was Jewish. In fact, some claim his religion (Jewish, Keynesian or both) likely cost him a tenured professorship at Harvard in the 1940s.

Like Edmond Halley's name, Samuelson's will forever be linked to one particular field of study—economics, in Samuelson's case, rather than astronomy. Also like Edmond Halley, many biographical tomes have been written about Paul Samuelson—and after his recent passing, I'm sure many more will follow. Can a mortal really summarize the life of a deity? Here goes.

Paul Samuelson was born on May 15, 1915, in uneventful Gary, Indiana, which was also the birthplace of another famous Nobel Prize-winning economist, Joseph Stiglitz, who was born in 1943 and took the coveted prize in 2001. Other famous non-economists from Gary are Michael Jackson and his siblings. (It's not clear if economists can moonwalk.)

During the Great Depression, Samuelson's family moved about 20 miles north, to Chicago, where Paul eventually enrolled at the University of Chicago—home of Milton Friedman and other conservative economic theorists. In his Nobel Memorial Prize official biography, Samuelson claimed that he was "born again" as an economist in early 1932 when he attended in his first lecture about Thomas Malthus. Although he was turned off by the Chicago school's blind defense of free and efficient markets (he called them schizophrenic), Samuelson's friendship and intellectual rivalry with Milton Friedman continued for the rest of his life.

In 1935, Samuelson earned his B.A. and headed east to Harvard where he earned his master's degree in 1936 and eventually his Ph.D.

in 1941. During his time there, he fell under the spell of the Keynesian approach to economics, which argues that governments *should* get involved in financial markets and *not* leave economic affairs to Adam Smith's invisible hand. In 1936, the British economist John Maynard Keynes published his revolutionary book, *General Theory*, and Paul Samuelson was the great American disciple who synthesized the classical and Keynesian approaches to economics. Keynes advocated government intervention to help stimulate (demand and) the economy, while people such as Milton Friedman and the Chicago school promoted a more hands-off approach.

Interestingly, Paul Samuelson often used the term "cafeteria Keynesian" to describe himself, claiming to pick and choose only what he liked from the theory. In fact, in 1960 he advised newly elected John F. Kennedy—as the United States was heading into a recession—to reduce taxes. Kennedy, the Democrat, was shocked at the advice, but convinced by Samuelson. And, although Kennedy himself didn't live to fully implement Samuelson's advice, his successor, Lyndon Johnson, did implement the tax cuts.

Paul Samuelson never really served in any formal political capacity in Washington or elsewhere. He wasn't the chairman of an economic council, a chief economist or a secretary of finance. In fact, he proudly quipped he'd never spent more than three consecutive nights in Washington because it might cramp his writing style. In spite of his low-visibility approach, his fingerprints and footprints (emphasis on foot) were all over the 1950s and 1960s economic scene.

As I mentioned earlier, most college freshmen around the world should be familiar with Paul Samuelson through his textbook. You might have used it yourself. And yet it is quite rare for someone so young, so early in his career, to write a successful textbook. When asked what motivated and prompted him to embark on what became an 18-edition voyage, he replied that his wife had given birth to triplet boys and he needed the extra money to be able to send 350 diapers to the laundry each week. Samuelson claimed he held a mortgage-burning party in Belmont, Massachusetts, soon after his first royalty check arrived from the publisher. Unlike Irving Fisher, his acerbic sense of humor was memorable and Twain-like.

Paul Samuelson was recognized as an economics prodigy very early in his career, and the awards soon followed. In 1947 the American Economics Association awarded him the inaugural John Bates Clark Medal, bestowed to economists under 40 and considered to be the second most prestigious award in the field. The first most prestigious award in economics is the Nobel Prize, which he was awarded in 1970 for his broad-ranging contribution to economic science. Paul Samuelson received the National Medal of Science from President Bill Clinton in 1996.

Remarkably, it was only in his 50s that Paul Samuelson turned his research attention to matters of finance, the stock market and asset allocation—the basis for this chapter's equation. His first published research in the field didn't appear until the late 1960s. In those articles he laid the foundations upon which Robert Merton and Myron Scholes built their famous option pricing equation, which garnered them Nobel Prizes.

Although each one of the seven heroes in this book is exceptional, I have a special attachment to Professor Paul Samuelson. In addition to the letter he wrote me in March 1997, I had the opportunity to briefly meet him and shake his hand—something I couldn't do with Fibonacci or Halley—at a financial research conference in October 2008. You might recall that this was a month of extreme stock market volatility, with the Dow Jones Industrial Average (DJIA) falling more than 20% during the month—just after the collapse of Lehman Brothers and the near-meltdown at AIG.

I took the opportunity to thank Paul Samuelson—sheepishly, after a 10-year delay—for the letter he'd sent me a decade earlier in 1997 warning about aggressive exposure to the stock market simply because "the odds look good in the long run." It all seemed so prophetic, in hindsight.

At the same conference Samuelson was asked about his own asset allocation and the performance of his stock portfolio—something I certainly did not have the chutzpah to ask—and his response, with a smile, was "no comment." I personally believe he didn't want to make us all feel bad. In fact, I wouldn't be surprised if he was short (i.e., sold before) the September 2008 financial crisis.

Unlike Irving Fisher, he practiced the prudence he preached.

CHAPTER 6

WHAT IS YOUR FINANCIAL LEGACY TODAY?

EQUATION #6: SOLOMON S. HUEBNER (1882–1964)

$$A_x = \sum_{i=0}^{\infty} \frac{(_i P_x)(q_{x+i})}{(1+R)^{i+1}}$$

In the early years of the 20th century, the North American life insurance industry suffered from a reputation far worse than today's tobacco, oil and gun industries. Apparently, executives at the largest insurance companies in the United States were paying themselves exorbitant sums of money and hiding their shenanigans by issuing fraudulent financial statements. Executives were bribing judges and politicians to keep their affairs secret.

The New York state legislature heard rumors of these matters and decided to conduct a formal investigation into the allegations in 1905.

The proceedings, which were a public relations disaster for the insurance industry, were led by New York Senator William Armstrong and Charles E. Hughes. The press loved the spectacle in which captains of industry were grilled about spending habits. Americans from all walks of life took a keen interest in the conspicuous consumption of insurance executives. Reading the media reports, I was reminded—100 years later—of the broad interest and disgust at the downfall of Enron and Lehman Brothers.

The Armstrong committee led to transformational reforms and eventually prohibited the sale of many (good) life insurance products, unfortunately a classic case of regulatory overreaction. The affair also made a celebrity out of the committee's chief counsel, Charles E. Hughes. He went on to become governor of New York, U.S. secretary of state, a Supreme Court justice and even a presidential candidate in 1916. Think of Eliot Spitzer going after Wall Street for its crooked financial dealings, then being elected governor as his reward.

The backlash against the insurance industry was fierce. For decades after, "insurance men" as they were called—and they were mostly men—were actually embarrassed to tell their mothers what they did for a living. Jokes of that sort still circulate in the industry.

Fast forward a full century, and although insurance companies get some bad publicity every now and then—think AIG— and people still tell jokes about insurance agents, the Armstrong investigation days are behind them. Today, most observers would agree: life insurance agents and brokers are no different from other professionals such as accountants, lawyers or doctors. They're members of a professional association who must comply with ethical guidelines, are heavily regulated, take qualifying exams, have continuing education requirements, etc.

The one person most responsible for rehabilitating the life insurance industry's image in the 1920s, '30s and '40s was a charismatic mid westerner from the "badger state" of Wisconsin by the name of Solomon S. Huebner. "Sunny Sol," as he was known, is probably the least famous of the seven pioneers I've profiled in this book. But to the insurance industry, he was a *bona fide* rock star. Think of him as the Elvis Presley or Mick Jagger of whole life, participating insurance policies. Although Huebner passed away more than 50 years ago, anyone who's been in the life insurance business long enough—and especially if they're good at it—knows and respects the legend.

Sunny Sol was no marketing guru. Nor was he a motivational speaker or insurance apologist doing battle with the media's insurance naysayers. To the contrary, Solomon S. Huebner was a full professor at the venerable Wharton School of Business. In the early 20th century, he was chairman and founder of its insurance department and author of seven textbooks and many scholarly articles. He was the first proper insurance economist, and is often called the founding dean of insurance education. In short, he was a scholar of insurance.

In addition to Huebner's day job teaching and supervising students, he traveled tirelessly around the country—and eventually the world—proselytizing about the importance of owning life insurance. He was particularly well regarded in East Asia, where the emperor of Japan awarded him an Order of the Sacred Treasure, a big deal there. (Interestingly, the Japanese have the world's highest ownership rate of life insurance.)

According to Professor Huebner's estimates—as reported by his biographer Mildred F. Stone—over a 40-year period he gave an average of one seminar or lecture *per day*.

Thanks in great part to Huebner's legacy, in 2010 more than 150 million North Americans owned individual life insurance with a death benefit of more than $10.5 *trillion* dollars. Today, life insurance companies have hundreds of billions of dollars in reserves, are respectable members of the financial services industry, and I venture to guess few executives have even *heard* of the Armstrong investigations.

This all ties into the bigger question I ask later in this chapter: Do you really need any life insurance once you've retired?

Human Life Value: *Raison d'être* of Life Insurance

In the beginning, around 17th-century England to be precise, life insurance was perceived as just another gamble, or a game of chance, involving three people. The *owner* of a policy paid (small) premiums to an insurance company that was obligated to pay the *beneficiary* a (large) death benefit if and when the *insured* died. In many cases the *owner* and the *insured* were the same person, but it didn't have to be that way. Sometimes the *owner* was also the *beneficiary*.

But, in contrast to fire or property insurance, life insurance—profiting from someone's death—was viewed with a jaundiced eye. The industry faced fierce opposition from the Church, which believed buying life insurance was a sin that showed a lack of faith in God. In many European countries, life insurance—betting on lives, as it was often called—was illegal.

In those countries where it was legal, not much thought was given to *how much insurance* people should own. During that period of time, the entire sales process itself was *ad hoc* and arbitrary. The Armstrong investigation certainly shattered any notion the life insurance industry operated a charity.

But then Solomon Huebner came along and transformed the marketing and sale of life insurance into a scientific discipline. He brought the tools of economics and human capital valuation into a field that lacked discipline and respect. He was the Frederick W. Taylor—the father of scientific business management—of the life insurance industry.

Here's how Professor Huebner phrased it in his classic book called *The Economics of Life Insurance*, first published in 1927:

> Economists have experienced difficulty in assigning to insurance a place in the science of economics. They have been accustomed to grouping economic activities under such time-honored classifications as production, exchange, distribution and consumption. Insurance has been to them a riddle, incapable of being assigned definitely to any one of these major divisions . . . (page 3)

Huebner's main idea, and the one for which he's recognized today, is the concept of *human life value* (HLV). This is just another way of saying human capital value, which I introduced in Chapter Five. The human life value is the present value of all the wages, salary and income a breadwinner will earn over the course of his or her working life. And, more importantly, it should be insured in the same way that property is insured. Put simply, if you're 45 years old, earn $50,000 per year and plan to retire at 65, your gross human capital is worth a cool million (20 × $50,000 = $1 million).

Here it is in Huebner's words:

> The economic value of human lives may be defined as the monetary worth of the economic forces that are incorporated within our being, namely, our character and health, our training and experience, our personality and industry, our judgment and power of initiative, and our driving force to put across in tangible form the economic images of the mind . . . (Huebner, page 5)

Huebner then went on to argue that as a result of high mortality rates among workers—in the early part of the 20th century, only six out of 10 workers alive at 25 reached the retirement age of 65—every head of household had a moral responsibility to buy life insurance to protect his family.

Huebner was quite forceful about his views, both in his writings and his lectures, citing the Spanish Flu of 1918 as an example of what lay ahead for the uninsured. In that epidemic, 675,000 Americans perished, most in their prime working years. Anyone who had purchased life insurance left a legacy for his family. Those who didn't left destitute widows and orphans.

Figure 6.1 displays the age dependent mortality rates around the period of the 1918 influenza. That pandemic involved a variant of the H1N1 virus that reappeared again with minimal damage in 2009, but killed millions of people globally, during the 1918 period. Notice that instead of the patterns that Benjamin Gompertz predicted for mortality, there is a large hump between the ages of 15 and 45, corresponding to prime working ages and child-rearing years.

What all this means is that instead of viewing the purchase of life insurance as a morbid gamble—a prevailing view still held by many—Huebner argued it was the opposite:

Not to insure adequately through life insurance is to gamble with the greatest economic risk confronting man. If understood, the gamble is a particularly selfish one, since the blow, in the event the gamble is lost, falls upon an innocent household whose economic welfare should have been the family head's first consideration . . . Failure to safeguard dependents is little short of a crime . . . (page 10)

Figure 6.1 U.S. Mortality Rates 1917–1919

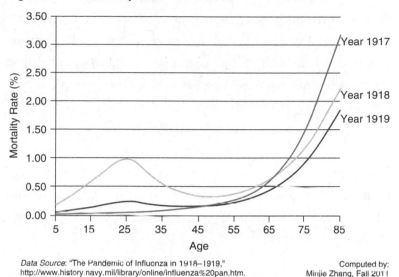

Data Source: "The Pandemic of Influenza in 1918–1919," http://www.history.navy.mil/library/online/influenza%20pan.htm.

Computed by: Minjie Zhang, Fall 2011

It's important to emphasize that although these statements seem quite routine from the perspective of the early 21st century, in Huebner's time such thinking was deemed radical. If you have seen or heard this argument during an insurance sales pitch, it is likely due to Huebner. When Huebner eloquently stated that "the capitalized worth of the earning power of a life is an economic asset, just as truly as property," the light bulb went on in the minds of life insurance executives still recovering from the shame and embarrassment of Armstrong. I'm sure they practically drooled when an esteemed professor at the world's leading business school went on to say:

> There are few callings, if any, which offer to the practitioner a greater opportunity for service than does life insurance. If pursued in a high-minded way, life insurance ranks in nobleness and possibility of service with the other time-honored professions . . . (page 18)

Professor Huebner founded the American College, in Bryn Mawr, Pennsylvania, which today awards the Chartered Life Underwriter (CLU) to professionals in the insurance industry. What's more, Huebner actually instituted an oath that CLU professionals must take today—similar to the Hippocratic Oath sworn by medical doctors and health professionals—to do no harm.

Yet, on the topic of the precise numbers for human capital value and the actual dollar amount of life insurance people should own, Huebner was less scientific. This was left to future generations of insurance economists and scholars, some of whom criticized him on this *vagueness*—a point I'll return to later. On this very point, Huebner himself stated:

> The question is often asked: Is there not some blanket formula for general application in the appraisal of life values for family insurance purposes? The answer is that there is no one royal road—one blanket formula—for such appraisals. Every family is a problem unto itself . . . (page 37)

What's the Most Effective Way to Create a Legacy?

Here's my main discussion point for this chapter.

While you're working, you must ensure your dependents and loved ones are properly taken care of in case you're no longer able to work. This is achieved with disability and unemployment insurance, and most importantly with life insurance. *Once you've retired, should you—and can you actually afford to—leave them anything by still paying for an expensive life insurance policy?*

Millions of retirees at advanced ages own some life insurance policy. Their goal? To create a legacy for their loved ones.

Often, however, that legacy requires that they continue paying premiums long after they've stopped earning a paycheck and can actually afford those premiums. Even if the policy is fully paid, there are often options for selling or cashing in the policy prior to death so the money can be enjoyed by the retiree or his/her dependents while both are still alive.

In the opposite case, retirees own valuable assets they're expecting to bequeath to their loved ones and in the meantime are living on income generated by those assets. Think of money in a bank account or a coupon-bearing bond where the intent is that these assets will form the principal part of the estate. The drawback is that the income is taxed quite highly and holding these investments within an insurance policy would be more tax efficient.

Many people are concerned about estate taxes or probate fees and other income taxes triggered by death from the sale of a cottage or a business. Indeed, that *could* also be a valid reason for owning an insurance policy well into your advanced years. But this can't be determined without a proper cost/benefit analysis. Nothing's free in life, especially when it comes to insurance. This leads us to the need for some mathematics.

Imagine this: your generous uncle has promised to give you $100,000 from his estate when he dies, but he is 66 and quite healthy. What is that promise worth today? Likewise, assume the same uncle has a life insurance policy with a death benefit he no longer needs or wants, perhaps because his formerly dependent children have grown up and are self-sufficient. He is thinking of somehow disposing of or surrendering the policy in exchange for some up-front cash now. What is a promised legacy (death benefit) worth today?

How do you calculate the *present value*—in the language of Fibonacci—of a sum of money your beneficiaries will receive at some random time in the future? This brings us to Equation #6.

Life Insurance: The Formula

Equation #6 enjoys many similarities to Halley's equation (Equation #3) for the value of a life annuity. They both involve a summation sign Σ, the probability of dying q_x, the probability of living $(_ip_x)$, and a periodic interest rate R. Indeed, these symbols and terms should be familiar from Gompertz, Halley and Fisher. What's more, to the untrained eye Equation #6 looks awfully similar to Equation #3.

Where this chapter's equation differs from Halley's annuity equation, however, is the focus on dying rather than living. Halley's equation provided the value of a series of small payments (a.k.a. an annuity) that *end upon death*. Now it's time to value one very large payment (a.k.a. a death benefit) *received by beneficiaries only at death*.

Moving on to the mathematics, the numerator in the equation, $(_ip_x)\,(q_{x+i})$, represents the probability of dying during age $(x+i)$, assuming you're actually alive at age x. This, once again, is quite different from Chapter Three's annuity equation, where the numerator represented the probability of living. The denominator of Equation #6 captures the interest rate R and the time value of money. All cash flows must be discounted to the present, from today until infinity (or at least until the policy terminates).

Here's a detailed example of how to value a five-year term life insurance policy at age 65.

This policy guarantees a $100,000 death benefit to your spouse or beneficiaries, but only if you die in the next five years. If you have

Table 6.1 The Present Value of a $100,000 Death Benefit

	Alive at Birthday Die Within Year (%)	Alive at Age 65 Survive to Year End (%)	(A) Alive at Age 65 Die During Year (%)	(B) PV $1 Factor at 5%	(C) Death Benefit ($)	(A x B x C) Product ($)
Age 65	1.06	98.94	1.06	0.9524	100,000	1,011
Age 66	1.18	97.77	1.17	0.9070	100,000	1,058
Age 67	1.31	96.49	1.28	0.8638	100,000	1,105
Age 68	1.45	95.09	1.40	0.8227	100,000	1,153
Age 69	1.61	93.56	1.53	0.7835	100,000	1,201

SUM: $5,528

the misfortune of dying one minute after your 70th birthday, the insurance company owes you nothing. This is what's meant by *term* insurance. In this case, the infinity sign in Equation #6 is replaced by the value of $N = 5$, representing the five years of coverage.

Table 6.1 breaks it all down. The first column represents the probability of dying within any given year, for example $q_{65} = 1.06\%$ between your 65th and 66th birthdays, or $q_{66} = 1.18\%$ between your 66th and 67th birthday, all the way until $q_{69} = 1.61\%$—the probability of dying after your 69th birthday but before your 70th birthday. If you're wondering where in the world someone gets these numbers, the answer is Benjamin Gompertz (remember him from Chapter Two?), or the mortality tables constructed by actuaries.

The second column in Table 6.1 represents the probability of surviving to a given age. Mathematically, if there's a 1.06% probability of dying before your 66th birthday—assuming you are 65 years old—there's a 98.94% probability of living to 66. The two must add up to 100% because there are no other alternatives!

Likewise, the probability that you, as a 65-year-old, will survive for two whole years—to 67—is the product of the individual probabilities of not dying in your 65th or 66th years. Mathematically this is $(1 - 0.0106)(1 - 0.0118) = 97.77\%$, the second number in that column.

Finally, the third column represents the probability a 65-year-old will die in any *given* year. For the first year it's the same 1.06%. For the second (66th) year it's the probability of living to 66 (which was 98.94%) multiplied by the probability of dying in that year (1.18%) leading to the value of 1.17%.

Notice a very subtle but extremely important point: if someone asked the question, *what are the chances of dying between your 66th and 67th birthday?*, the answer would depend on your current age *right now*. Sure, if you're already 66 the probability (first column) is 1.18%, but if you're still 65 there's a chance you might not make it to 66—which is why the probability is (only) 1.17% in column 3. The difference is formally known as conditional versus unconditional probabilities.

Now, my intent here is not to convert you into statisticians or actuaries—just to offer a flavor of the complexity involved in such calculations. Bear with me, we have one more step.

Back to Equation #6 and the final step. You multiply the columns ($A \times B \times C$) together—death rate times present value factor times death benefit value—then add up the numbers and you get the value of a $100,000 death benefit. The value of such a policy is $5,528 assuming the given mortality rates and the 5% interest rate. Remember, Equation #6 is expressed per $1 of death benefit. Since the death benefit is $100,000 we multiply everything by 100,000.

To be clear, this chapter's equation is an attempt to estimate: i) what a fully paid life insurance policy is worth, and ii) how much it might cost today to purchase an insurance policy, in one lump sum, promising a $100,000 death benefit. As there are many different ways to finance such a policy, such as paying monthly premiums, you must be careful how you interpret this particular equation. I'll return to this subtle point later.

Here's yet another way to think about it.

If your 65-year-old uncle (or grandparent or long-lost relative) pledges his $100,000 five-year term life insurance policy's death benefit to you, don't spend the $100,000. In fact, don't spend more than $5,528. Because that's all it's worth. Personally, if I were given the choice—being risk averse—I'd take the $5,528 cash and tell Uncle Generous to pledge the policy to someone else.

Okay, but what if Uncle Generous is 70, 75 or 80? More importantly, what if the policy is not term but permanent, which is also called whole life? And how does the answer depend on the 5% rate I assumed? Read on.

More Examples: Different Ages

Table 6.2 uses the same equation—but with a spreadsheet to handle all the numbers—to compute the discounted value of a $100,000 death benefit, under a variety of interest rates and at various ages. In this case, I assumed the policy is permanent. In other words, it

Table 6.2 The Value of a $100,000 Death Benefit at These Ages

Age →	50	55	60	65	70	75	80	85	90
Valuation Rate (%)									
1	$72,609	$75,973	$79,340	$82,640	$85,921	$88,773	$91,417	$93,683	$95,530
2	$53,367	$56,348	$63,538	$68,830	$74,099	$79,158	$83,827	$87,935	$91,000
3	$39,733	$45,319	$51,370	$57,776	$64,362	$70,894	$77,097	$82,697	$87,474
4	$29,983	$35,610	$41,936	$48,870	$56,236	$63,765	$71,114	$77,914	$83,841
5	$22,945	$28,315	$34,569	$41,656	$49,422	$57,592	$65,780	$73,538	$80,442
6	$17,814	$22,787	$28,775	$35,778	$43,682	$52,229	$61,014	$69,528	$77,258
7	$14,034	$18,560	$24,184	$30,959	$38,823	$47,552	$56,742	$65,846	$74,273
8	$11,221	$15,300	$20,519	$26,985	$34,691	$43,459	$52,904	$62,459	$71,471
Life Expectancy	32.6	28.0	23.6	19.4	15.6	12.1	9.1	6.6	4.6

covers you for life and the summation in Equation #6 is from zero all the way to infinity.

For example, the value of a permanent $100,000 death benefit at age 65, under a 5% valuation rate, is $41,656. This is much more than the $5,528 value from Table 6.1 because—as I mentioned—this policy lasts your entire life rather than merely five years. In all likelihood a (live) 65-year-old will die after his or her 70th birthday, when the five-year policy would have expired. Hence the large difference between $5,528 and $41,656. Uncle Generous, who makes you the beneficiary of his permanent policy (lasting forever instead of a limit of five years), is giving you something worth $41,656. Hopefully this is intuitive.

Notice how the numbers in Table 6.2 change as a function of current age, x in the equation, and the rate R. If the rate is lower, say 3%, the actuarial value of the policy is $57,776. This is over $16,000 more than the previous case because when interest rates are lower all present values are higher. You need more today to create the same sum of money later. This goes back to Fibonacci's time value of money, Equation #1.

Likewise, if the valuation rate is higher, for example 8%, the actuarial present value of the $100,000 death benefit is a mere $26,985 instead of the $41,656 under the 5% rate. The intuition is exactly the same. With higher rates, present values are lower. Also, notice the impact of age. If Uncle Generous is 80 (under a 5% interest rate), the value is $65,780 because he's more likely to die sooner. As you can see from the final row in the table, life expectancy at age 80 is only 9.1 years, whereas at 65 it's 19.4 years. At 80, the Grim Reaper is closer.

If You Try This at Home

For those readers who actually want to try using Equation #6, consider a number of caveats before playing amateur actuary:

1. Life insurance usually pays off a few days after the insurance company receives a copy of the death certificate (notwithstanding the occasional rumor that insurance companies lose the mail and keep the money for themselves). The formula assumes cash flows are made and death benefits are paid at the end of the period. This period can be one week, one month or one year. So, for example, Table 6.1 assumed if Uncle Generous passed away, you'd only get the death benefit at the end of the year. That's how the discounting was set up. If you wanted to value a real, live insurance policy, you'd have to create a more refined grid for the mortality rates. Table 6.1, for example, would then have 12 × 5 = 60 rows, if you wanted to approximate monthly payments.

2. Table 6.2 assumes a permanent life insurance policy, purchased at various ages and under various interest rates, assuming continuous-time payments. In other words, it accounts for the possibility you can die anytime and the company would immediately pay the death benefit. Technically, Equation #6 is being used with daily mortality rates. This is a very long summation, which is why you might not get the exact numbers listed in the table.

3. The underlying mortality rates I used for Tables 6.1 and 6.2 are exactly the same as those used in the Gompertz chapter (Chapter Two), namely $m = 87.25$ and $b = 9.5$. In practice, depending on health status, one might use different rates. For example, if Uncle

Generous is 65 but healthy as a horse, perhaps you should treat him as 55 for the sake of valuing the insurance policy; conversely, if he's overweight and smokes, you might treat him as 75. In other words, Uncle Generous's biological and chronological ages may not coincide. It may be best to ask his doctor, rather than relying on the age on his birth certificate. Insurance companies use their own mortality estimates when pricing insurance.

4. I emphasize, again, that all the numbers above apply to a fully paid policy, meaning all your premiums have long ago been paid. If you're still paying premiums, subtract the actuarial present value of the premiums to be paid from the numbers in Table 6.2 to arrive at the proper value. Alternatively, consult an actuary.

This discussion of death and death benefits can seem rather cold and off-putting, and I completely understand that you may be feeling uncomfortable with it. Legacies are more than money, and the death of a loved one isn't something to joke about. But that's exactly the point of this chapter. One of the seven most important conversations about retirement involves whether life insurance is the most effective way to achieve your legacy objectives.

As we've seen, making your daughter a beneficiary on a $100,000 insurance policy doesn't mean she's getting $100,000 in today's dollars. The actuarial present value is much, much lower. Remember, a dollar today is worth much more than a dollar to be received in twenty years. Vice versa, if you have $100,000 in the bank and you're living off the interest only but would like the principal to go to your loved ones upon death, there might be more effective ways of doing that with life insurance. Have the conversation and use the equation!

He Wasn't a Quant

I should make absolutely clear that unlike those who invented or discovered the other equations presented in this book, Solomon Huebner did not invent or discover Equation #6. In fact, actuaries had been using mathematical techniques to value, price and set aside reserves for life insurance policies in the United States, the United Kingdom and Europe for decades before Huebner came along in the early 20th century.

For the most part, Huebner shied away from the mathematics of insurance. And he was most definitely not an actuary. His 1927 book on the economics of insurance, revised in 1944 and again in 1959, began with:

> The present volume is not intended to present the highly technical aspects of life insurance, such as the home office [insurance company] might desire. Instead, its purpose is to emphasize the economic services of life insurance, a subject ... which has unfortunately been greatly subordinated in previous publications, to the mathematical principles ... (page viii)

Historically, the American Society of Actuaries (SoA), founded in the 19th century, began administering exams on insurance pricing techniques in 1896—well before Huebner arrived on the scene. The educational textbooks and material from the SoA have expressions similar to Equation #6 for valuing life contingencies.

I'll leave it to the historians of actuarial science to debate whether Richard Price (in 1783), William Morgan (in 1779) or Francis Bailey (in 1810) got there first. But if you are really interested in the origin of Equation #6, you might consult the definitive 10-volume compendium by the British actuary, Professor Steven Haberman (a good friend of mine) and Trevor Sibbett on the history of actuarial science; fine bedside reading.

In my humble opinion, if anyone deserves credit it should be Edmond Halley, who mused about the valuation of life insurance, as well as annuities, in his famous paper—written in 1693. You see, technically, if you can value a life annuity you can value a life insurance policy. They are opposite sides of the same coin, and there's a strict mathematical (i.e., no arbitrage) relationship between the two.

In sum, what Solomon Huebner deserves full credit for is legitimizing, promoting and rehabilitating Equation #6—and the industry that stood behind it.

Secondary Markets and Life Settlements

Here's yet another reason Equation #6—and the conversation around life insurance—is so important for proper retirement income planning.

Over the last two decades, thousands of Americans conducted the equivalent of a financial garage sale, and—after many years of ownership—decided to sell their life insurance policies to complete strangers with the help of a specialized broker. For some, it was to a large group of strangers; for others, it was to one individual. Collectively, these strangers took over the responsibility for making any premium payments if the policy had not been fully paid; equally, the same strangers became the beneficiaries of the policy. Thus, instead of the death benefit money going to the insured's spouse, kids or grandkids, it would go to Mr. Stranger.

This process—which may seem distasteful to many—unlocked billions of dollars in extra cash for the original policyholders who couldn't afford to wait until dying to collect the proceeds. In Irving Fisher's words, and to put it mildly, the owners were very impatient.

Now, whether or not you intend to sell your insurance policy, or whether it makes financial sense for you, depends in part on *what number you're being offered* in relation to Equation #6. If at 65 the stranger is offering you $50,000 for a $100,000 death benefit and you're in good health, it's not a bad deal. If they only offer you $5,000, run away!

Evidence suggests, however, that most people aren't getting the best price relative to the actuarial value of their death benefit (i.e., Equation #6). A number of independent studies have examined offers made to policyholders and have questioned if most would be better off waiting for a better deal.

Now, all this might seem rather esoteric, but I believe this trend—secondary market sale of insurance—will continue growing, since many baby boomers, with no other means of financing their retirement, will have no choice. In fact, some in the industry project the secondary market could grow tenfold, to $150 billion (face value) per year by 2015 from the current $15 billion per year.

I believe Solomon Huebner would be greatly chagrined and dismayed to see this. Trading in life insurance policies was probably not what he had in mind, but I suspect he'd be amused that his beloved life insurance was being treated like just another financial asset.

Term versus Whole Life

Nowadays, some of Huebner's enthusiasm for (expensive) insurance that includes investments and savings has been tempered by the *buy-term-and-invest-the-difference* (BTID) philosophy. According to this popular view, the human life value declines toward zero at retirement, so there's no need for any life insurance in retirement. Any savings should be realized outside a life insurance policy. This view explains why, these days, almost 35% of insurance sales are of the term variety. Once the term is over, the coverage is done. Anything less or more is a waste.

In my personal experience, espousing the BTID philosophy to a crowd of well-compensated insurance agents is tantamount to blasphemy. After swearing and crossing themselves, Huebner's memory is quickly invoked in the defense of permanent versus term insurance.

Interestingly, a mere four years after Solomon Huebner died (he passed away on July 17, 1964), two eminent professors of insurance at Huebner's Wharton School wrote the following critical remarks in a leading scholarly journal devoted to life insurance research:

> The mass market, in fact, needs little or no insurance after 65. It may need savings, but these savings may take any form, of which insurance is only one alternative. Insurance to produce liquidity, tax advantages and other incidental benefits is generally not a high priority in the mass market . . . Huebner's conception of life insurance as the center of the investment process is now as outmoded as the view of the world before Copernicus . . . (*JRI*, 1968, page 353)

Ouch! Academics can be a nasty bunch.

But Sunny Sol Was a Fan of Annuities Too

Although most students of the industry rightfully view Huebner as a huge advocate of permanent and everlasting life insurance, he was actually a jack-of-all-trades. He wrote a popular textbook about the stock market and was recognized as a leading expert on marine insurance. He was instrumental—as a consultant and expert witness to the U.S. Congress—in creating the regulation governing the country's commerce and shipping.

But Huebner actually had quite a bit to say about retirement and life annuities—another reason he's one of the privileged seven in this book. It seems that his master plan was to have a policyholder convert some of his/her life insurance into a life annuity around retirement age. My interpretation of Huebner's writings is that life insurance wasn't meant to be owned until death. Rather, the intent was to convert it into something else. This can actually be done quite easily—if you have some cash value in the policy—with no adverse tax consequences, by exchanging the insurance into an annuity.

When you think about it, this is perfectly consistent with Huebner's thinking about human life value. While you're working, that income-generating potential must be protected. Once you're retired, it should be enjoyed by purchasing yet another product—annuities—sold by insurance companies, which Huebner also wrote about:

When the age of retirement is reached, it is important that the retiring worker be financially self-sufficient so that the heavy financial burden of old age support be not lodged upon his children, thus denying to them, as is now so often the case, their normal opportunities in life . . . Insurance proceeds may be converted into a life annuity . . . (Huebner, page 10)

It's interesting that Huebner's argument involved more than just mortality credits and insurance economics. Echoing Jane Austen, he also wrote:

Annuitants are long livers. Freedom from financial worry and fear, and contentment with a double income, are conducive to longevity. If it be true that half of human ailments are attributable at least in part to fear and worry, then the effectiveness of annuities for health and happiness must be apparent. I am inclined to believe that annuities serve in old age,

much the same economic purpose that periodic medical examinations
do during the working years of life. (Huebner, page 138)

I venture to guess that if Solomon Huebner were alive today and
still giving public lectures, he'd be on the road with annuity wholesal-
ers, giving seminars to financial advisors and their clients and singing
the virtues of longevity insurance and life annuities. I can assure you
he'd be compensated handsomely!

Solomon Huebner's understanding of retirement income challenges was quite prescient. Many economists and financial experts
have puzzled over the minimal appetite consumers have for life
annuities. I discussed this briefly in Chapter Three. The aversion to
annuitization is often called the *annuity puzzle* by economic researchers. It's puzzling due to a result first shown by Professor Menahem
Yaari in 1965. He extended Fisher's work on the lifecycle and proved
annuities are the most efficient method for de-accumulating (and
enjoying) wealth in retirement. The economist Franco Modigliani, in
his Nobel Prize-winning speech in 1985, helped focus the profession's
attention on the puzzlingly low demand for annuities, and hundreds
of research papers have followed.

But, indeed, the annuity puzzle was also recognized—and puzzled
over—by Huebner in the 1930s, before any formal model of the lifecycle was properly developed by economists.

The prospect, amounting almost to a terror, of living too long makes

necessary the keeping of the entire principal intact to the very end, so

that as a final wind-up, the savings of a lifetime, which the owner does

not dare to enjoy, will pass as an inheritance to others. In view of these

facts, it is surprising that so few have undertaken to enjoy without fear the fruits of the limited competency they have succeeded in accumulating. This can be done only through annuities. . . . Why exist on $600, assuming 3% interest on $20,000, and then live in fear, when $1,600 may be obtained annually at age 65, through an annuity for all of life and minus all the fear . . . (Huebner, page 140)

As far as I'm concerned, this is yet another reason to include Huebner as one of the seven intellectual giants on whose shoulders 21st-century retirement income planning research stands.

The Historical Huebner versus Fisher

Solomon Huebner was born on March 6, 1882, in Manitowic, Wisconsin. His parents were successful and prominent farmers of German descent and he learned the value of hard farm work through his childhood. He grew up under the influence of the Lutheran and Methodist churches, regularly attending church, Bible study and prayer. Partially as a result of the family's religious beliefs, Huebner's father didn't own any life insurance—but he did own insurance policies to protect against fire and other natural hazards, an ever-present risk for farmers living off the land. (I guess everyone's faith has limits.)

Solomon excelled in school, graduating top of his class, and was ready for university by age 13. He received his bachelor's and master's degrees from the University of Wisconsin, where he studied with and was influenced by the important American economist Richard T. Ely. Upon graduation, after traveling briefly in Europe, he received a scholarship to the University of Pennsylvania, where he earned his Ph.D. in 1905. Quickly recognized as an academic star, he was promptly asked to join the Wharton faculty where he launched the insurance department and was based until his retirement in 1953.

It's worth noting that his younger brother, Grover Huebner, followed him to the University of Wisconsin and then the University of Pennsylvania. Sol was known for his outspokenness, red neckties and made-up middle initial—S., as he decided to add "Stephen" to his name—while Grover was more reserved and quiet. Ultimately, the two served together on the Wharton faculty for decades—without much evidence of sibling rivalry. It's no wonder the name Huebner is so closely affiliated with that business school. On a quick side note, I actually spent part of my academic sabbatical at Wharton's insurance department where it was hard to miss all the monuments to the Huebner legacy.

One can't help but compare and contrast Solomon Huebner to Irving Fisher. Both were born around the same time, grew up in religious households, were academic economists and served as professors at Ivy League institutions. They traveled and lectured widely, were activists for public health and life conservation and enjoyed generous compensation for their speaking and consulting efforts. Moreover, it seems *they were interested in the exact same personal financial issues.*

Yet there's no evidence Huebner and Fisher ever met, knew each other personally or even cited each other's research work. This is quite odd since the 1920s and 1930s were a period of great fame, public outreach, government work and media activity for both men. One can only speculate they must have at least heard of one another.

I like to imagine they indeed did cross paths at some anonymous hotel conference center, or perhaps a train station, each on his way to address an audience keenly awaiting a lecture. Perhaps they exchanged a polite word or two regarding economic matters of the day and then went off to cash in on their human capital value.

Despite the superficial similarities, there were some important differences between these two giants. Fisher was a professor at Yale but spent very little time in the university's pedagogical affairs. He didn't have students who continued his legacy or were deeply devoted to him. He was an academic loner whose research work was highly mathematical and inaccessible to many economists of his era.

In contrast, Huebner fought hard to get the economic profession *interested* in the study of insurance. He was intimately involved in the management of the Department of Insurance at the Wharton School. He molded the department and kept tight control on all aspects of the curriculum. He was first and foremost an educator and teacher. Quite appropriately, his 1960 biography by Mildred Stone—a student of his—was called *The Teacher Who Changed an Industry*.

Whereas Fisher lost his life savings in the stock market crash of 1929, for Huebner the episode proved rather profitable. According to his biographer, he held most of his money in ultra-safe life insurance policies—as one might expect. Huebner was opposed to speculation, leverage and buying stock on margin, especially with money you couldn't afford to lose. Today, he'd most certainly disapprove of exotic options such as derivatives and triple inverse exchange traded funds.

Yet soon after the 1929 stock market crash, while prices were depressed, Huebner said to his wife, Ethel Elizabeth, "For once I'm going to do what I've always described to my students. Things are sinister, dark and discouraging. Now is the time to buy stocks." He then invested thousands of dollars—equivalent to hundreds of thousands today—across many different companies. He claimed, "One share in fifty companies is better than fifty shares in one company, because it gives the spread of averages" (Stone, page 257). Huebner profited handsomely from this diversification philosophy back in 1930, which coincidentally is the year Professor Harry Markowitz, the Nobel laureate—the founder of modern portfolio theory who is widely credited with inventing the mathematics of diversification—turned three.

Not bad for an insurance man.

CHAPTER 7

IS MY CURRENT PLAN SUSTAINABLE?

EQUATION #7: ANDREI N. KOLMOGOROV (1903–1987)

$$P\lambda_t = \frac{\partial P}{\partial t} + (\mu w - 1)\frac{\partial P}{\partial w} + \frac{1}{2}\sigma^2 w^2 \frac{\partial^2 P}{\partial w^2}$$

ndrei Nikolaevich Kolmogorov was a textbook Russian of the early 20th century with the ultimate Marxist-Leninist resume. For starters, his mother, Maria, and aunt, Vera, were both imprisoned by the Tsarist regime in the late 19th century. Legend has it that his family hid outlawed revolutionary literature under Andrei's crib when he was a baby. His father—a scientific agronomist—worked for the communist government, formed after the revolution in 1917.

ANDREI N. KOLMOGOROV (1903–1987)

Kolmogorov grew up in Yaroslavl, near the banks of the Volga River, and attended a gymnasium, which is a type of specialized high school. He then enrolled in Moscow State University in 1920, where he studied mathematics and physics, as well as Russian history and communist thought. He was recognized as a mathematical prodigy when he managed to prove certain *divergent Fourier series,* not supposed to exist in theory, could be found in practice quite easily. (Trust me, this is a big deal in mathematics.)

Kolmogorov was also an avid and passionate outdoorsman. His meetings with students and colleagues would often take place high atop some mountain outside Moscow, or in a canoe on the Volga River. It is said that he'd swim for hours in frigid Russian lakes in the dead of winter and was also known for skiing long distances in his shorts (some say underwear) through the snow-covered forest around his house in Komarovka, well into his 70s. Perhaps you have seen the (uncanny) pictures of Russian president Vladimir Putin, bare-chested atop a horse, arching a bow and arrow, hunting fowl. Well, he probably took his lead from Kolmogorov.

On the scientific dimension, Andrei Kolmogorov is considered a deity among mathematicians, and the only god among Russian mathematicians. He contributed to many fields of mathematics and physics, but is most famous for his foundation work in probability theory. Some have gone so far as to claim that what Euclid was to geometry, Kolmogorov was to probability. And, though he wrote and lectured primarily in Russian and German, most of his groundbreaking books and articles have long been translated into every modern language.

True to the socialist sprit, Kolmogorov didn't just focus his attention on the pure sciences. He used his statistical skills to research, and then publish, articles on the metric structure of poems by great Russian poets such as A.S. Pushkin as well as his 1920s contemporary Vladimir Mayakovsky.

Soviet honors and accolades came frequently. Kolmogorov was granted the Stalin Prize in 1941, the Hero of Socialist Labor award in 1963, the Order of the October Revolution in 1983, and the Order of Lenin an astounding *seven* times between 1944 and 1975. (Note that Fidel Castro and Josip Tito only received *one* each.) He won the Lenin Prize—an even bigger deal—in 1965.

When Kolmogorov died in 1987, his obituary in the newspaper *Izvestia* described him as a "model of nobility, unselfishness and moral purity in the service of his socialist homeland." This glowing tribute was signed by none other than then-Soviet leader Mikhail Gorbachev.

It is then supremely ironic that financial advisors at venerable capitalistic American institutions such as Goldman Sachs and Merrill Lynch owe Kolmogorov an incalculable debt of gratitude. You see, his work on probability theory—which I'll soon discuss—created the foundations for today's retirement income-planning tools. Every time a Wall Street–based American stockbroker runs a "Monte Carlo Simulation" to help a client achieve the very non-socialist goal of retiring rich, the client is indebted to Andrei Nikolaevich Kolmogorov.

Karl Marx and Vladimir Lenin must surely be turning in their mausoleums.

Will Your Retirement Plan Work Out?

Here's the current state of your retirement affairs.

In Chapter One you learned how to link your *fixed* spending rate in dollars together with the *fixed* interest rate you earn on the invested money to the number of years the money will actually last.

A simple tradeoff was quantified. In reality, of course, nothing is fixed—especially the number of years you spend in retirement. That's why in Chapter Two you learned about the randomness of human life and how that can be quantified. With a knowledge of longevity risk in hand, in Chapter Three you learned about the value of a pension annuity, which should—I argued—serve as the foundation of any retirement income plan. In Chapter Four you had a chance to ponder your patience and prioritize whether you want a constant spending rate for the rest of your life or are willing to trade off and accept some longevity risk. Chapter Five discussed the stock market and how to "think" about your asset allocation as a function of age and time. Then, Chapter Six discussed the value of a death benefit and how much is it worth today? Finally, in this definitive chapter, we bring it all together and ask: Assuming you have set a plan in motion—taking all the above uncertainties into account—what is the *probability your retirement plan is sustainable?*

A Purely Imaginary Case to Help

Moshe is 67 years old and married to Edna, 65 (who doesn't look a day older than 43). The year is 2035 and, finally, Moshe is about to retire. The couple estimates it needs approximately $70,000 per year to live comfortably, which, after a long discussion with Irving Fisher during a trip to Connecticut, they understand should be adjusted yearly for inflation. The couple is extremely averse to longevity risk and would like to maintain a $70,000 standard of living for life. The couple is unwilling to enjoy more today in exchange for less later.

The $70,000 number, of course, is after tax. Moshe estimates the couple would require a gross income of $100,000 so they can actually enjoy (and consume) the $70,000 after all income taxes are paid. To be clear, the $100,000 amount is often called the *dollar-valued withdrawal rate*.

Moshe and Edna are also entitled to a government Social Security pension and a private-sector Defined Benefit (DB) pension from Moshe's employer. Their Social Security income generates a total of $20,000 per year, adjusted for inflation. But Moshe's employer's DB plan is more complicated; the plan allows him to elect a lump sum (today) of $400,000 or receive a lifetime pension annuity of $35,000 per year, also adjusted for inflation.

The couple is unsure about whether to take the lump-sum cash value or the life annuity since they already have the aforementioned $20,000 government pension entitlement. Ideally, Moshe and Edna would rather have the ability to take half the lump sum and half the pension annuity, but his DB plan (like most others) doesn't offer this option. It's an all-or-nothing decision. What to do?

To help figure things out, the couple consulted Edmond Halley and Benjamin Gompertz over fine biscuits and English tea. Gompertz pointed out that Edna, the younger (and healthier) of the couple, would likely live much longer than Moshe. Said Gompertz to Moshe, "Your force of mortality will always be much higher than Edna's so, to be safe, you should base all your retirement income planning on her age, although there is a non-zero probability that you might outlive her." The DB pension annuity guarantees $35,000 as long as either of them is still alive.

For his part, Halley noted that the $35,000 pension would be worth at least $500,000, if not more, according to his equation's calculations. In his view, the $400,000 lump-sum offer would not adequately compensate for giving up the $35,000 inflation-adjusted pension annuity.

Following the discussions with Gompertz and Halley they were almost convinced, but the couple decided to consult Solomon Huebner over cognac and cigars. They worried that should they take the annual $35,000 pension (instead of the $400,000 lump sum payment) and something happened to them both in the near future, the money would be lost to their kids and grandkids. Under such a circumstance, how would they create a financial legacy for their loved ones?

Huebner's advice was quite emphatic.

"First," he said, "pension annuities are the most efficient way to spend down capital." He warned the couple that if they took the lump sum they'd always live in fear of spending principal and would be gambling with their nest egg. Second, if legacy was a concern, Huebner recommended Edna purchase a permanent life insurance policy for a few hundred thousand dollars. She was in excellent health and would likely qualify for preferred rates. He also gave them the phone number of some insurance agents he knew.

And so, with the backing of all these luminaries, Moshe and Edna decided to take the pension annuity of $35,000 for their retirement. Remember, though, this doesn't cover all their annual expenses. They wanted $100,000 (pre-tax), and are receiving $35,000 + $20,000, which is $55,000 in pension income, leaving a gap of $45,000, or 45% of their needs. How is the deficit financed?

Luckily, they were very prodigious savers during their working years (okay, Moshe more than Edna) and managed to accumulate $900,000 in a tax-sheltered retirement savings account. Their plan? To withdraw the $45,000 per year from the $900,000 nest egg. Will it last?

To get the answer, they invited Leonardo Fibonacci over to dinner for some pasta, wine and rabbit *foie gras*. Right away, he recognized the dilemma they faced and quickly pointed out that if—and it was a big if—they knew exactly what rate their investments would earn for the remainder of their lives, he could easily tell them how long the money would last. "At 1% constant and real interest, the money will last for 22.3 years, at 2% money runs out in 25.5 years, and if you can get a constant 3% real interest rate every year, you have 30.5 years of steady cash-flows."

Moshe and Edna told Fibonacci their investment portfolio wasn't earning a fixed rate. It was neither 3% nor even 1%, but instead quite random and unpredictable; in some years the return was actually negative (taking inflation into account). Furthermore, they wondered if 30 years was even enough. They didn't quite know what interest rate to use in Fibonacci's equation, or how to interpret the results in a world in which life itself is random. "Sorry," said Fibonacci. "That sounds like stochastic stuff, which is far ahead of my time."

So Moshe and Edna paid a visit to famed economist Paul Samuelson, long since retired and enjoying condo living in Sunny Isles Beach, Florida. "We're retiring and don't have time to recover from any stock market losses," said Edna and Moshe. "How much risk should we take with our precious nest egg?" Samuelson's response was rather curt. "Retirement age has nothing to do with it, and neither does time," he said, echoing his extensive writings. "It's all about financial risk aversion. As Harry S. Truman said, 'If you can't handle the heat, stay out of the kitchen.'"

Having received this rather tautological response from the famed Nobel laureate, and wondering whether the trek to Florida was worth it, they turned and asked a final question. "Okay, if we invest in a balanced investment portfolio that is 60% stocks and 40% bonds, will we be able to maintain our standard of living? Will our portfolio be ruined if we get some bad years in the market before the good years return?"

"Well, I don't believe in using ruin probabilities as a measure of risk," said Samuelson. "That's best left to gamblers. I thought I warned you about that fallacy in the 1990s. But if you insist, you should contact a Russian mathematician named Andrei Nikolaevich Kolmogorov."

From Monte Carlo to Netherlands, Sweden and then Russia

Imagine you're visiting the casinos of Monte Carlo, Las Vegas or Macau, and having fun at one of the roulette wheels. Your strategy is quite simple and cheap. You only bet on black, and with each spin of the wheel you only bet $1. Accordingly, if the wheel lands on black you get $2, and if the wheel lands on red you get nothing—losing your dollar. To make things easier, let's ignore greens and say you started the evening with $100. You plan to leave the casino as soon as one of two things occurs: i) either you double your money to $200, or ii) you lose your entire $100 (i.e., you're ruined).

Here's the question: What's the probability your $100 capital will reach zero before it reaches $200? This one's relatively easy since it's a 50/50 proposition. But what if the odds are skewed against you (as in most casinos)? Or what if you plan to leave only when you reach $300 or $500 in capital? And what if you take some money off the table to buy a drink every few rounds? This gets more complicated and requires some serious mathematics.

In fact, this is quite the famous question in the theory of probability and is known by the moniker of *Gambler's Ruin problems*. Its study dates back almost four centuries. The formal computation of ruin probabilities begins in the 17th century, with Christiaan Huygens (1629–1695), a Dutchman, who first formulated and solved the problem I just posed. This led to many further developments in probability theory, most notably by Pierre-Simon Laplace (1749–1827).

The first person to apply *ruin probability mathematics* to actuarial science, and specifically to practical insurance company problems, was a Swedish actuary named Filip Lundberg (1876–1965). In his 1903 doctoral dissertation, Lundberg applied the work of Huygens and Laplace to the cash flows of an insurance company. On a roulette wheel, black could be thought of as insurance premium inflows, and red as insurance claims. The odds of an insurance company going bankrupt were akin to the odds of reaching zero during a night at the casino. Today, Lundberg's work—which was popularized by another Swedish actuary, Harald Cramer (1893–1985)—is taught to actuarial students around the world (or at least it should be).

Now, back to retirement. If you think about it carefully, there's a strong similarity between the process of gambling on a roulette wheel—your money going up and down—and the process of investing and spending during retirement. The difference between them is: i) your portfolio moves up and down continuously, and depends on the stocks and bonds you've selected, and ii) you're spending money from this portfolio, which increases the chances your portfolio will shrink in value over time. This leads to a much more complicated mathematical ruin problem evolving in continuous time, and brings us back to Professor Kolmogorov.

The Equation Itself Is Only Partial

Warning: the next page involves some concepts from calculus which are important for *understanding* the equation, but aren't necessarily required to *apply* the equation. Feel free to skip ahead if you want.

You should notice a few different and unusual things about Equation #7.

First, it doesn't quite look like the other six. This one's expressed as a *differential* equation, as opposed to a *regular* equation. By differential equation I mean that instead of relating the ruin probability (P) to the risk/return, spending rate and mortality rate parameters, it relates their *derivatives* (a.k.a. rates of change) to each other. This means that although you can use Equation #7 to confirm you have the correct answer, you can't use it directly to obtain the correct answer itself. I'll return to this distinction.

To start, let's examine the parameters and variables in this *differential equation*:

1. Instead of using biological age (x), we'll operate in retirement time (t). Think of it as daylight savings time: once you retire, time begins anew.

2. The probability of lifetime ruin, defined as the probability you'll live longer than your money, is denoted by (P). This is the main number we're after.

3. The instantaneous force of mortality (IFM), is the death rate at time t, denoted by the symbol λ_t. Over relatively short periods of time, denoted by ε (measured in years), the IFM can be approximated by: $\lambda_t = -ln[_\varepsilon p_t]/\varepsilon$. For example, if you're 65, which is retirement time $t = 0$ then according to the Gompertz law of mortality ($m = 87.25$, $b = 9.5$) the probability of surviving for one month ($\varepsilon = 0.08333$ years) is 0.999153. The negative of the natural logarithm of this number, divided by the same $\varepsilon = 0.08333$, leads to an instantaneous force of mortality of $\lambda_0 = 0.010163$. This is a death rate of

approximately 1% per year. But, at age 70, which is retirement time $t = 5$, the corresponding value is $\lambda_5 \approx 0.017203 = -ln[0.998567]/(\frac{1}{12})$, a death rate of approximately 1.7% per year.

4. The probability of lifetime ruin is an explicit function of retirement time (t) and the amount of money you have *relative* to the amount you're planning to spend, denoted by (w). So if you've saved $1 million and plan to spend $45,000 (pre-tax) from this portfolio per year, then $w = \frac{1,000,000}{45,000} = 22.223$ *wealth units*. Likewise, if you're lucky enough to have $2 million in savings, and plan to spend $90,000 per year, the ratio, and hence the value of w, is the same. All that matters is the ratio.

5. The derivative (a.k.a. rate of change) of the probability with respect to time is denoted by $\frac{\partial P}{\partial t}$, the derivative with respect to wealth is denoted by $\frac{\partial P}{\partial w}$ and the second derivative with respect to wealth is denoted by $\frac{\partial P}{\partial w^2}$. If you have no idea what a *second derivative* means, not to worry.

6. The expected return of the investment portfolio is denoted by μ (for example, 5% per year), and the volatility or standard deviation of the portfolio is denoted by σ (for example, 15% per year). Note: you should be familiar with both of these parameters from the discussion in Chapter Five.

Here it is in words.

Equation #7 states the ruin probability multiplied by the instantaneous force of mortality must be exactly equal to the sum of three distinct terms. The first term is the derivative of the ruin probability with respect to time. The second term is the difference between the dollar-valued return minus 1, multiplied by the derivative of the ruin probability with respect to wealth. The third term is the second derivative of the ruin probability with respect to wealth, multiplied by the wealth times volatility squared, all divided by two. Yes, exhausting and quite a mouthful. That's why mathematicians use abbreviated symbols.

Later on I'll confirm that the numbers listed in the tables actually satisfy Equation #7 by adding up these three terms and comparing their sum to the left-hand side. But first, here are some actual examples.

Detailed Example

Let's get back to our earlier story.

Edna is a 65-year-old retiree planning to withdraw $45,000 (real) from the couple's $900,000 investment portfolio, invested in funds containing 60% stocks and 40% bonds. Over the last 50 years, such a 60/40 portfolio has earned approximately 5% after inflation, but with a volatility of 15%. This means that 67% of the time, it earned between 5% + 15% = 20% and 5% − 15% = −10%. So we use the numbers $\mu = 5\%$ and $\sigma = 15\%$ in the equation. In short, she's spending $45,000 per $900,000, which is an initial withdrawal rate of exactly 5%.

According to Table 7.1, the probability the nest egg will be exhausted while Edna's still alive is 19.37%, nearly 20%. This is the lifetime probability of ruin. Thus, there's an 80% chance her standard of living is sustainable. (The two—ruin plus sustainability—must add up to 100%.)

Is this good or bad? Well, let's see. Recall that 55% of the couple's income needs are covered with 100% certainty (from pensions). The other 45% is exposed to some risk, and only has an 80% chance of being sustainable. Weigh the two together and you get:

The sustainability of Moshe and Edna's original retirement income plan is: (100%)(55%) + (100% − 20%)(45%) = 91%

Table 7.1 Lifetime Ruin Probability with Balanced Portfolio

Probability of Survival to End Of...	Spending Wealth	6.45% $15.50	6.06% $16.50	5.71% $17.50	5.41% $18.50	5.13% $19.50	5.00% $20.00	4.88% $20.50	4.65% $21.50	4.44% $22.50	4.26% $23.50	4.08% $24.50
	Age											
98.94%	65	36.06	31.50	27.45	23.89	20.78	19.37	18.07	15.71	13.68	11.92	10.39
98.82%	66	33.92	29.49	25.59	22.17	19.20	17.87	16.63	14.41	12.49	10.84	9.43
98.69%	67	31.77	27.49	23.74	20.47	17.65	16.39	15.22	13.14	11.35	9.81	8.50
98.55%	68	29.63	25.50	21.91	18.81	16.14	14.96	13.86	11.91	10.25	8.83	7.62
98.39%	69	27.49	23.53	20.11	17.18	14.68	13.57	12.54	10.73	9.19	7.89	6.78
98.21%	70	25.38	21.60	18.36	15.60	13.26	12.23	11.28	9.61	8.20	7.00	6.00
98.01%	71	23.29	19.71	16.66	14.08	11.91	10.95	10.08	8.54	7.25	6.17	5.26
97.80%	72	21.25	17.87	15.02	12.62	10.62	9.74	8.94	7.54	6.37	5.40	4.58
97.55%	73	19.26	16.10	13.44	11.23	9.40	8.60	7.87	6.61	5.56	4.68	3.96
97.29%	74	17.34	14.39	11.95	9.92	8.25	7.53	6.87	5.74	4.80	4.03	3.39
96.99%	75	15.50	12.78	10.53	8.69	7.19	6.54	5.95	4.94	4.11	3.44	2.88

Note how I've taken the weighted average of the income silos—55% pension income, 45% portfolio withdrawals—and weighed them by the probability that each source is sustainable. All else being equal, the more income you receive from *pensionization*™ sources, the greater the sustainability of your retirement plan. By *pensionized* I mean that the income source is guaranteed for life.

To make sure this is clear, here's another example.

Let's go back to Moshe and Edna and assume that instead of spending $100,000 (pre-tax) they decide they can live on an income of $91,688 (pre-tax). Accordingly, the $55,000 pension income will cover 60% of their retirement income needs, and the other 40% (which is $36,688) must be withdrawn from the $900,000 nest egg. This is an initial withdrawal rate of $36,688 divided by $900,000 which is 4.08%, which is lower (and safer) than the original 5%. The couple's investment portfolio and retirement time remains the same. According to Table 7.1, the lifetime ruin probability of the investment portfolio (upper-right-most corner) is 10.39%, approximately 10%. Putting this all together, we arrive at:

The sustainability of Moshe and Edna's revised retirement income plan is: (100%)(60%) + (100% − 10%)(40%) = 96%

No surprise here. Their retirement sustainability is 5 percentage points higher because Moshe and Edna plan to spend less during their retirement. In fact, if they were to delay their retirement withdrawals by a few years, to age 70 or 75, for example, they'd score even higher. Notice that the farther down the table you look, the lower the ruin probability, which conversely leads to a higher sustainability value. This should all be rather intuitive.

Table 7.2 provides some alternative values for the ruin probabilities, the main ingredients for the sustainability calculation. In

Table 7.2 Lifetime Ruin Probability with High-Risk Portfolio

Probability of Survival to End Of...	Spending Wealth											Age
	6.45% $15.50	6.06% $16.50	5.71% $17.50	5.41% $18.50	5.13% $19.50	5.00% $20.00	4.88% $20.50	4.65% $21.50	4.44% $22.50	4.26% $23.50	4.08% $24.50	
98.94%	39.92	36.71	33.80	31.16	28.76	27.65	26.59	24.63	22.84	21.21	19.73	65
98.82%	38.17	35.01	32.15	29.57	27.24	26.16	25.13	23.22	21.49	19.92	18.50	66
98.69%	36.38	33.28	30.48	27.97	25.70	24.66	23.66	21.82	20.15	18.64	17.28	67
98.55%	34.56	31.52	28.80	26.36	24.16	23.15	22.19	20.42	18.82	17.37	16.07	68
98.39%	32.71	29.75	27.11	24.74	22.63	21.65	20.73	19.03	17.50	16.12	14.88	69
98.21%	30.85	27.97	25.41	23.13	21.10	20.16	19.28	17.65	16.20	14.89	13.71	70
98.01%	28.98	26.19	23.72	21.53	19.58	18.69	17.85	16.30	14.92	13.68	12.57	71
97.80%	27.10	24.41	22.04	19.94	18.08	17.24	16.44	14.97	13.67	12.51	11.46	72
97.55%	25.23	22.65	20.38	18.38	16.62	15.82	15.06	13.68	12.46	11.37	10.40	73
97.29%	23.38	20.91	18.74	16.85	15.19	14.43	13.72	12.43	11.29	10.27	9.37	74
96.99%	21.54	19.19	17.14	15.36	13.80	13.09	12.43	11.22	10.16	9.22	8.39	75

this case I've used Equation #7, assuming a much more aggressive portfolio, one that's invested 100% in stocks. Having a higher equity allocation (from 60% to 100%) allows me to use a higher expected investment return μ in Equation #7, but to compensate for the extra risk involved I must use a higher volatility σ. In the case of Table 7.2, I assumed the portfolio was expected to earn 7% after inflation in any given year, but that investment returns would fluctuate by 25%. Technically speaking, this is a (geometric mean) growth rate of approximately 4% per year.

Notice the ruin probabilities displayed in Table 7.2 are uniformly (consistently) higher than the values listed in Table 7.1. For example, if your initial withdrawal rate is 5% ($45,000 from a $900,000 portfolio) the ruin probability is now 27.65% instead of the 19.37% in Table 7.1. This is a full 8 percentage points higher because of the increased risk. The extra 2 percentage points of investment return (7% versus 5%) can't offset the additional 10 percentage points of volatility (25% versus 15%.) The tradeoff isn't worth it.

Of course, if the ruin probability is higher, the sustainability of the retirement plan will be lower. For example, under Moshe and Edna's original plan, the plan's sustainability would be (100%)(55%) + (100% − 28%)(45%) = 87.4%. This is almost 4 percentage points lower, compared to the balanced portfolio displayed in Table 7.1. (Note that I'm using a higher 28% ruin value to weigh withdrawals from the investment portfolio.) Hopefully you have a sense of how to get the lifetime ruin probability first, then use that to balance the sources of income and obtain a weighted average sustainability quotient.

Just to make sure this is clear, here's a final (extreme) example. Let's assume Moshe and Edna decided to take the lump-sum payment offered by their pension plan, which you recall was $400,000. They add this to their $900,000 portfolio so their retirement capital consists of $1.3 million, which is invested 60% in stocks and 40% in bonds. This might seem like a large sum of money, but recall they'd like to spend $100,000 (before tax) every year and their only source of guaranteed income is the $20,000 Social Security. In this case, 80% of their desired income must be sourced and withdrawn from their investment portfolio. Withdrawing $80,000 from a $1.3 million portfolio is equivalent to an initial withdrawal rate of $(80/1300) = 6.15\%$. The lifetime ruin probability for a 6.15% withdrawal rate is approximately 33%. Putting this all together, we get that their sustainability—if they take the lump sum instead of the pension—is $(100\%)(20\%) + (100\% - 33\%)(80\%) = 73.6\%$. Notice how much lower this number is compared to the earlier 91%. This is the benefit of pensionization(™).

Also, note that I place 100% sustainability weight on the income from the lifetime pension annuity. This would only apply if I was absolutely 100% certain the entity standing behind the pension promise was: i) free of any risk of default, and ii) would continue to pay that income—adjusted for inflation—for the rest of their lives. Those are two big "ifs" indeed, and if you worry about such things, you are perfectly justified in using a number smaller than 100% to weight the pension income.

Verification that Kolmogorov's Equation Is Satisfied

There's one final thing, assuming you haven't abandoned me yet: to confirm the numbers in the table actually satisfy Kolmogorov's *differential* equation, Equation #7.

Now, in earlier chapters I confirmed an output number was correct by inserting some parameters into the equation's right-hand side, then comparing values with the left-hand side. With a *differential* equation, however, this can't be done in exactly the same way. This is because the main number—the probability of lifetime ruin—isn't given explicitly, thus requiring a slightly different means of verification. To confirm a *differential* equation, you must gauge how the numbers *change* with increasing values of time and wealth. I'll pick one particular point on the grid within Table 7.1 and see if it "moves" by the direction and magnitude predicted by Equation #7. Hang on. You'll see what I mean.

Look at Table 7.1, and in particular the number listed for age 65 and a wealth level of $20. The probability of ruin is 0.1937493, displayed with only four digits and in percentage terms as 19.37%. If you move down the column to age 66, at the same $20 wealth level, the ruin probability is reduced to 0.1786661—listed as 17.87%. Intuitively, the probability is lower because it represents a retiree who is a year older (66 versus 65) and has the same amount of money in her retirement account. Hence, she is in better financial shape. The difference between these two numbers (17.87% − 19.37%), divided by the difference in time between the ages of 65 and 66, is −0.015083 units. This value is an approximation for the time derivative of the ruin probability and the first of *four* important quantities required for verification. It's the first term on the right-hand side of differential Equation #7.

The next (second) important quantity I need is $(\mu w - 1)\partial P / \partial w$, the product of the derivative of the ruin probability ($\frac{\partial p}{\partial w}$), multiplied by something called the diffusions *drift* term ($\mu w - 1$). I'll start with the first derivative ($\partial P / \partial w$). This is approximated by subtracting the ruin probability at wealth $w = \$20.50$ (age 65), from the ruin probability at wealth $w = \$20$ (and same age 65), then dividing by the difference in wealth between the two points—or $0.50. Do the math and this works out to −0.026160 units. The reason the derivative is negative is because the ruin probability declines the wealthier you are at retirement. (Makes sense, no?) Then, we multiply −0.026160 units by $((0.05)(20) -1)$ to arrive at the second important quantity of the verification process, which is simply 0. This might seem like considerable effort for a zero, but the 5% times 20 equals exactly 1—only at this point on the grid. If the wealth value happened to be lower than $20, the relevant quantity would be negative; vice versa if it was larger than $20.

The third quantity on the right-hand side of Equation #7 is the product of the second derivative of the ruin probability $(\partial P^2 / \partial w^2)$ and the squared volatility (σ^2) times the wealth squared (w^2), all divided by two. Let's tackle the easy part first, and compute $(0.5)(0.15)^2(20)^2 = 4.5$ units. Moving on, the (more cumbersome) second derivative with respect to wealth is approximated as follows.

I'll compute the first derivative—as earlier—at two different points, $w = 20.00$ and $w = 19.50$, then divide the difference between those two numbers by the difference in wealth level, $0.50.

Here goes. The first derivative (approximated) at $20 is −0.026160. The first derivative (approximated) at $19.50 equals −0.028065. The difference between these two (first derivatives) divided by 0.50 wealth units is 0.00381 units. Finally, we arrive at the right-hand side of Equation #7. It's $−0.015083 + 0 + (4.5)(0.003810) = \mathbf{0.00206}$.

And, here's the last step.

The left-hand side of Equation #7 is the probability of ruin itself at the point of $w = \$20$, or $P = 0.1937493$ multiplied by the instantaneous force of mortality (IFM) rate, λ_0 at age 65. This is retirement time $t = 0$. As explained earlier, the IFM can be approximated by the (negative of the) natural logarithm of the survival probability and dividing by the increment in time, i.e., the one year from age 65 to 66.

Notice, from the left-most column in Table 7.1, the probability of surviving from 65 to 66 is 0.98938, 98.94%. This leaves $\lambda_0 \approx - \ln[0.98938] = 0.010670$ as the instantaneous force of mortality at age 65. Finally, multiply 0.1937493 (the survival probability) by 0.010670 (the mortality rate) to arrive at **0.00206** for the left-hand side. *Voilà!* Kolmogorov's equation is confirmed. (I'll leave the confirmation of Table 7.2 as a homework assignment.)

A side note: this differential equation is useful and quite relevant even if you use a statistical (a.k.a. Monte Carlo) simulation to measure your retirement's sustainability. Kolmogorov provides you with an audit procedure and a sanity test. Equation #7 can help confirm that the values you're getting from a simulation are correct. Namely, to test your "simulation engine," generate a lifetime ruin probability for two adjacent wealth values (slightly wealthier versus slightly poorer) and one adjacent time value (slightly older versus slightly younger) and using the procedure I described above, confirm they satisfy Equation #7—or are close. If not, something's wrong.

Physics, Not Finance

Andrei N. Kolmogorov published more than 500 scientific research articles during his life, supervised and guided more than 70 graduate students and made profound contributions to almost every branch of mathematics. But he never dabbled in mathematical finance and most of his work in probability theory—including the famed Equation #7—was intended as a contribution to theory.

The original paper on which Equation #7 is based was published in 1931 under the German title of "Uber die analytischen Methoden in der Wahrscheinlichkeitsrechnung" (no, I can't pronounce that either) in the venerable *Mathematical Annals*. This paper formulated the connections between differential equations and probability and gave rise to the theory of modern stochastic (a.k.a. random) processes.

Kolmogorov's 1931 paper introduced the concept of a *continuous time* and *continuous state-space* Markov process. A Markov process—named after another famous Russian mathematician, Andrei Markov (1856–1922)—is a collection or a sequence of random variables whose outcomes are unaffected by the past. Think roulette wheel or coin tosses.

More importantly, in his 1931 paper, Kolmogorov derived a differential equation for the transition probabilities that such a continuous Markov process—moving from one state to another—would have to satisfy. What this means (in English, to us) is that he was able to obtain the probability that your investment portfolio, if you modeled it as a Markov process, would grow 10% by next Wednesday, lose 50% at some point during the next decade or *hit zero before you die*. Kolmogorov taught the world how many important problems in probability can be solved by finding the relevant differential equation that contains the answer.

Note, carefully, that the equations for the transition probabilities are based on the assumption the process was not subject to discontinuous and/or predictable jumps. This, then, is a critical assumption in using Equation #7. If you don't believe your portfolio will move continuously (or can be approximated as such), or if you think you can outguess the market using technical analysis because you see "head and shoulder" patterns whenever you stare at Dow charts, then you aren't entitled to use Kolmogorov's Equation #7. He won't let you.

On a historical note, most MBA students of finance are likely familiar with the name Kiyosi Ito (1915–2008) as it relates to modern finance. Ito was the first mathematician to construct a stochastic differential equation (SDE), which is a very powerful way of describing a random process and is the foundation for modern option pricing. Some might wonder about the connection between these two giants. At the risk of getting technical, Ito's key contribution was to teach the world a new calculus of how to work with random processes based on their sample paths. But getting mathematicians to accept his construction was not possible until he proved that transition probabilities actually obeyed Kolmogorov's equations. In a sense, Ito had to go through Kolmogorov to get his calculus approved, and there is a legendary story of the two meeting in the late 1970s at a conference in their honor.

Note also that Gambler's Ruin (or retirement ruin) was never the motivation for Kolmogorov's differential equation. It's but one of the many important applications of his contributions to probability. His work is useful in many different fields of science, from modeling Mendel's genetic laws to the study of fluid mechanics. In fact, he was more than just an ivory tower theorist. To study ocean turbulence, Kolmogorov joined a naval expedition as its chief scientific officer— just like Edmond Halley almost 300 years earlier. And, during the Second World War, Kolmogorov was asked to use these equations to predict the paths of ballistic weapons. In that context, the probability of ruin is more ominous.

Back to Andrei Nikolaevich Kolmogorov

Much of what has been written about Kolmogorov's personal life—as well as a substantial part of his own writing—is in Russian and has yet to be translated into a language that I can read. Fortunately, I've had the opportunity to speak to a number of his former students. I was able to piece together the rest from the obituaries of ANK—as he was commonly known, in honor of the character from Tolstoy's *War and Peace*—and what emerges is a rather unusual and often traumatic story.

Kolmogorov's biological mother, Maria Kolmogorova, died immediately after giving birth to him, on April 25, 1903. The infant was then brought to the village of Tunoshna on the banks of the Volga and raised by his aunt, Vera. His father, Nikolai Kataev, never formally married his mother Maria, and didn't seem to be much involved in the boy's upbringing. Unfortunately he too died, when Andrei was a mere 16 years of age, during the 1918 Civil War.

In 1942 Kolmogorov married Anna Dmitrievna; he knew Dmitrievna from his student days. They never had any children. Some claim he married her solely to save her from the Soviet gulag and possible death, as her first husband had recently been arrested as a traitor. This is unconfirmed. Kolmogorov did, however, have an adopted son from Anna's first marriage. Coincidentally, he also became a teacher of mathematics.

In terms of companionship, most of Andrei's life was spent with his partner and colleague, Pavel Sergeyich Alexandrov—also a distinguished mathematician. The two purchased a country home in the village of Komarovka in the 1930s and spent much time together working on mathematical papers and books, meeting their graduate students and hosting international colleagues. Today, their house and the library in which he worked is a treasured historic site. Think of it as the Russian mathematicians' "Hall of Fame."

Despite Kolmogorov's impressive stature and connections, his academic life wasn't free of controversy or stress. His fame brought international invitations to lecture and publish his research in scientific journals around the world. This was frowned upon by the die-hard Soviets who felt all science should remain in Mother Russia. Moreover, in an era of rampant communist-sponsored anti-Semitism, Kolmogorov openly and vocally encouraged Jewish students. In 1980, he was awarded the Wolf Foundation (Israel) Prize for mathematics—one of the highest awards given in Israel, enraging his anti-Semitic detractors.

On the educational side Kolmogorov was intimately involved and interested in the education of young children. In the early 1960s he helped establish a dedicated school—fondly called the Kolmogorov School, but officially known as Resident School #18—where youngsters were exposed to the equivalent of mathematics and physics immersion. Many went on to become successful and prolific mathematicians. Surprisingly, in this too Kolmogorov faced criticism from members of the Soviet academy and party, because the textbooks he used in the school weren't deemed suitable.

One can certainly chalk up any criticisms to petty academic battles, against the crumbling background of a paranoid communist hierarchy, but it had real implications for Kolmogorov's health. These battles were fought in the government controlled media, reached deep into the Soviet party hierarchy and led to numerous academic tribunals—a uniquely Soviet phenomenon.

Sadly, Professor Kolmogorov died in a Russian hospital after a very long battle with Parkinson's, on October 20, 1987, at 84. Ominously, he died a few hours after the notorious world stock market crash, which took place the day before, on October 19. That event was an early warning sign—heeded by few until 2008—that market prices don't follow continuous paths. A probabilistic coincidence? Maybe. One thing's certain: the legacies of both—Kolmogorov and the crash—live on among the quants.

CONCLUSION

CONTROVERSIES, OMISSIONS AND CONCLUDING THOUGHTS

Getting an equation named after you isn't easy. Unlike a building, hospital ward or even a business school, money can't buy you this sort of fame. Being brilliant, or a genius, is necessary but probably not sufficient for equation immortality. You need to be a good communicator and very prolific. Having many students to build on your breakthroughs certainly helps. But most importantly, you must own a very sharp set of knives.

A number of our seven champions spent the latter part of life defending their claims to originality. In many cases the waters were muddied regarding who got there first, and it's only with the passage of time that historians have bestowed the credit posthumously.

For example, there are some historians who claim the 5th-century Indian Sanskrit text *Aryabhatiya* should be properly credited for introducing the decimal system to the world, or that the ancient

Chinese deserve credit for many of the ideas attributed to Fibonacci. In fact, *Liber Abaci* was lost for many years and there are still those who are skeptical he actually invented the technique for computing the time value of money.

In 1832, an Englishman by the name of T.R. Edmonds started a vicious letter-writing campaign to discredit Benjamin Gompertz and his famed law of mortality. Edmonds claimed he had discovered an earlier and better version. In the end, leading mathematicians and actuaries rallied to Gompertz's defense, and history (as well as this book) gave him proper credit.

In 1671, more than 20 years before Edmond Halley published his contribution to annuity pricing, a Dutchman by the name of Jan de Witt achieved something of a scoop, only discovered many years later. He published an article entitled "Value of Life Annuities in Proportion to Redeemable Annuities" in which he derived an expression very similar to Equation #3. In fact, de Witt was no ivory tower academic. He was actually the prime minister of Holland at the time. Can you imagine that? It's hard to visualize a modern prime minister having the time for such things, especially since Holland was at war with France at the time. But de Witt's equation didn't take into account realistic mortality population rates in the way Edmond Halley did in his article. This is why Halley gets the final credit in this book and according to most actuaries—though Dutch actuaries understandably have a slightly different verdict.

While on the subject of the Dutch, I must admit that I strongly considered including the Dutch astronomer Christiaan Huygens' equation for the Gambler's Retirement Ruin probability as one of the seven. But I felt that one astronomer (Edmond Halley) was enough, and Kolmogorov has taken the field far beyond the simple rules of binomial probability.

Speaking of actuaries, most would deny credit to Solomon Huebner for any technical contribution, although his mastery of insurance and lasting contribution to the industry are undeniable. As you saw in Chapter Seven, even the great Andrei Kolmogorov had to battle and sling mud with some of his Russian comrades.

As I said earlier, money isn't enough when it comes to naming an equation.

What Equations Are Missing?

Some readers might wonder about other famous equations that have not been profiled or even mentioned in this book. Students of finance will wonder about the option pricing equation developed by the economists Fischer Black, Myron Scholes and Robert Merton. Likewise, every business student is taught about the capital asset pricing model (CAPM) equation developed by William Sharpe. The equation for the efficient investment frontier developed by Harry Markowitz is the bread and butter of all modern mutual funds. And all these esteemed scholars went on to win the Nobel Prize in economics for their work. So why weren't they budgeted one of the seven slots?

The answer is threefold. First, I believe these "finance" equations have already received enough fame (and fortune) elsewhere. The classic 1993 book by Peter Bernstein, *Capital Ideas: The Improbable Origins of Modern Wall Street*, did a wonderful job of merging the fascinating history and the foundational equations of finance. More importantly, the financial crisis of 2008 has raised serious doubts about the validity of these equations in predicting or forecasting market prices. Finally, and most importantly, I was not convinced those equations were directly relevant to *retirement income* planning. Remember, this book was meant to be about conversations (and calculations) that take place around the topic of retirement income. So, despite the elegance and fame of option pricing formulas, I consciously decided not to include them in this book.

That said, if you think I omitted an important equation—or if you have a dog in this race—please let me know. I'm not sure if this book will make it to 18 runs like Samuelson's, but there's always the possibility of a second edition!

APPENDIX

CRASH COURSE ON NATURAL AND UNNATURAL LOGARITHMS

I'm sure it has been many years (decades?) since you were in high school, so allow me to refresh your memory about the *natural logarithm function* and its mirror image, the *natural exponent function*. Both functions—or buttons on your calculator, if you like—feature prominently in the most important equations of this book. Natural logarithms are actually close cousins to *common* (or base 10) logarithms. I'll explain the connection in a moment.

First, the notation I use for the *natural* logarithm of any number n—for example, the number 15, 2 or 0—is the expression $ln[n]$. That is the letter l, the letter n and then square brackets containing the number you would like to "lon" (which is how it is pronounced). In parallel, the notation I use for the *natural* exponent of any number n is the expression e^n. Any good business or scientific calculator has a *function button* that converts numbers into their natural logarithm and/or can then reverse the process to recover the original number. Okay, now let me explain what the buttons do.

You might remember your common (base 10) logarithm, which is based on the same idea. The common logarithm (pronounced "log") is another button on your calculator. One is LN and the other is LOG. The common logarithm of any number x is equal to the value—call it y—such that 10 to the power of that y recovers the original x. For example, the common logarithm of $x = 100$ is $y = 2$, because 10 to the power of 2 is 100. Likewise, the common logarithm of $x = 1000$ is equal to $y = 3$, because 10 to the power of 3 is 1,000. You can do this with negative numbers as well. The common logarithm of $x = 0.1$ is equal to $y = -1$, because 10 to the power of -1 is $\frac{1}{10}$ which is the original 0.1 number. Here it is again, the common logarithm of $x = 0.001$ is $y = -3$, because 10 to the power of -3 is $\frac{1}{1000}$ which is equal to 0.001, etc. See Table 1 for additional numbers.

Now, the *natural* logarithm uses a *base* of 2.7183 instead of the base of 10, but the power idea is exactly the same. I'll explain why the number 2.7183 is so special in a moment. First, let me offer some numerical examples.

As you can see from the third column in Table 1, the *natural* (base 2.7183) logarithm of the number $x = 1$ is $y = 0$, because 2.7183 to the power of 0 is equal to 1. Likewise, the natural logarithm of $x = 5$ is equal to $y = 1.6094$ because the number 2.7183 to the power of 1.6094 is exactly equal to the original 5. Finally, the natural logarithm of the number $x = 0.01$ is equal to $y = -4.6052$, because 2.7183 to the power of -4.6052 is equal to 0.01.

Now, to be precise, although I said the base is 2.7183, that's only the first five digits of the true number I was using. The actual number is very, very long. It's called irrational—which means it can't be written as a ratio of two integers—and there's no regular or repeating

Table 1: Logarithms from Base 10 to Base e

Original Number	Logarithm Base 10	Logarithm Base 2.7183
0.000	-00	-00
0.001	-3.000	-6.9078
0.010	-2.000	-4.6052
0.100	-1.000	-2.3026
0.500	-0.301	-0.6931
1.000	0.000	0.0000
1.100	0.041	0.0953
2.000	0.301	0.6931
2.7183	0.434	1.0000
5.00	0.699	1.6094
10.00	1.000	2.3026
100.00	2.000	4.6052
1000.00	3.000	6.9078

pattern to the numbers. (Google e if you want to get the next million digits.) To avoid writing a very long number every time it's needed, mathematicians have decided to use the letter e to denote this (rather beautiful) base number. Thus, using proper notation, $e^0 = 1$ and at the same time $ln[1] = 0$. Hopefully, this is all starting to make sense and brush out the cobwebs.

The nice thing about natural logarithms—and for that matter, any logarithm—is that the natural logarithm of a product is equal to the sum of the individual logarithms. For example, $ln[20] = ln[10] + ln[2] = 2.3026 + 0.6931 = 2.9957$. This means that $e^{2.9957} = 20$, by reversing the same process.

Who cares? Well, historically, before calculators and personal computers came on the scene, this relationship was a true godsend. If you had to multiply two very large numbers, all you had to do was get the logarithm value of each—readily available in old logarithm tables—add them up, and then invert (raise to the power of the base) to obtain the product you wanted. Nowadays, with the invention of modern spreadsheets and scientific calculators—and the generally pathetic state of numeracy—the popularity of logarithms has declined. But they still arise in many places in nature, including retirement planning!

The last thing I still must explain is what is so special (or *natural*) about this number $e = 2.71828\ldots$ and why it shows up repeatedly in so many of our financial equations. Well, here goes.

I was surprised and amused the first time I saw this. Hopefully you will be as well.

Imagine that you invest \$1 at exactly 100% annual interest rate. How much money will you have at the end of the year? Well, the mathematics of this one is rather trivial. $1 \times (1+1) = 2$. So you have \$2. But what if the 100% interest you are getting is compounded twice per year? In other words, you get 50% in the first six months and then 50% in the second six months. In that case, the formula would be $1 \times (1.5)(1.5) = 2.25$, which is an extra 25 cents. The reason for the extra interest is the increased compounding period. After six months you have \$1.50 and then 50% interest on that grows to \$2.25 in total.

Now what happens if you compound quarterly? In that case the proper expression would be $1 \times (1.25)(1.25)(1.25)(1.25)$, which can be written as $(1 + \frac{1}{4})^4 = 2.4414$, which is an extra 44 cents compared to annual compounding. What about weekly compounding? The final number would be $(1 + \frac{1}{52})^{52} = 2.6926$ dollars. Do you see a pattern here yet? Let's do daily compounding. This leads to $(1 + \frac{1}{365})^{365} = 2.7146$ dollars at the end of the year. And finally, what happens if the bank compounds your interest every second of the day? For the record, that is 31,556,926 seconds in a year. The number you need is $(1 + \frac{1}{31556926})^{31556926}$.

You guessed it: you end the year with 2.718282 . . . or exactly e. Yup. This is why e pops up all over finance, money and economics. It truly is a remarkable number, and justifiably embedded in the DNA of the most important equations for retirement.

REFERENCES AND SOURCES

Chapter 1: Leonardo Fibonacci

C.M. Brown (2008), *Fibonacci Analysis*, Bloomberg Press, New York.

K. Devlin (2011), *The Man of Numbers: Fibonacci's Arithmetic Revolution*, Walker Publishing Company, New York.

L. Eisenberg (2006), *THE NUMBER: A Completely Different Way to Think About the Rest of Your Life*, The Free Press, New York.

W.N. Goetzmann and K.G. Rouwenhorst, editors (2005), *The Origin of Value: The Financial Innovations that Created Modern Capital Markets*, Oxford University Press, New York.

W.N. Goetzmann (2003), *Fibonacci and the Financial Revolution*, working paper, Yale University International Center for Finance.

R.E. Grimm (1973), "The Autobiography of Leonardo Pisano," *Fibonacci Quarterly*, Vol. 11, No. 1, February, pp. 99–104.

G. Poitras (2000), *The Early History of Financial Economics: 1478–1776*, Edward Elgar Publishing, Northampton.

L. Sigler (2002), *Fibonacci's Liber Abaci: A Translation into Modern English of Leonardo Pisano's Book of Calculation*, Springer Verlag, New York.

P. Zima and R.L. Brown (1993), *Mathematics of Finance* (4th Edition), McGraw-Hill Ryerson, Toronto.

Chapter 2: Benjamin Gompertz

J.F. Carriere (1994), *An investigation of the Gompertz law of mortality*, Actuarial Research Clearing House.

D.C.M. Dickson, M.R. Hardy and H.R. Waters (2009), *Actuarial Mathematics for Life Contingent Risks*, Cambridge University Press, Cambridge.

B. Gompertz (1825), "On the Nature of the Function Expressive of the Law of Human Mortality, and on a New Mode of Determining the Value of Life Contingencies," *Philosophical Transactions of the Royal Society*, Vol. 115, pp 513–585.

P.F. Hooker (1965), "Benjamin Gompertz," *Journal of the Institute of Actuaries and Assurance Magazine*, Vol. 91, pp. 203–212.

R.D. Lee and L.R. Carter (1992), "Modeling and Forecasting U.S. Mortality," *Journal of the American Statistical Association*, Vol. 87(419), pp. 659–671.

H. Maier, J. Gampe, B. Jeune, J.M. Robine and J.W. Vaupel (2010), *Supercentenarians*, published by Springer Verlag, Berlin.

W.M. Makeham (1890), "On the Further Development of Gompertz's Law," *Journal of the Institute of Actuaries*, Vol. 29, pp. 316–332.

J. Oeppen and J.W. Vaupel (2002), "Broken Limits to Life Expectancy," *SCIENCE*, Vol. 296, pp. 1029–1031.

S.J. Olshansky, B.A. Carnes and C. Cassel (1990), "In Search on Methuselah: Estimating the Upper Limits to Human Longevity," *SCIENCE*, Vol. 250, pp. 634–640.

S.J. Olshansky and B.A. Carnes (1997), "Ever Since Gompertz," *Demography*, Vol. 34(1), pp. 1–15.

J.H. Pollard (1991), "Fun with Gompertz," *GENUS*, Vol. XLVII, pp. 1–18.

S.D. Promislow (2011), *Fundamentals of Actuarial Mathematics* (2nd Edition), John Wiley and Sons, Ltd, United Kingdom.

Human Mortality Database. University of California, Berkeley (U.S.), and Max Planck Institute for Demographic Research (Germany). Available at www.mortality.org or www.humanmortality.de (data downloaded on 1 October 2011).

Chapter 3: Edmond Halley

G. Alter and J.C. Riley (1986), "How to Bet on Lives: A Guide to Life Contingent Contracts in Early Modern Europe," *Research in Economic History*, Vol. 10, pp. 1–53.

J.E. Ciecka (2008), "Edmond Halley's Life Table and Its Uses," *Journal of Legal Economics*, Vol. 15(1), pp. 65–74.

J.E. Ciecka (2008), "The First Mathematically Correct Life Annuity Valuation Formula," *Journal of Legal Economics*, Vol. 15(1), pp. 59–63.

A. Cook (1998), *Edmond Halley: Charting the Heavens and the Seas*, Clarendon Press, Oxford University Press, New York.

M.V. Fox (2007), *Scheduling the Heavens: The Story of Edmond Halley*, Morgan Reynolds Publishing, Greensboro, North Carolina.

W.N. Goetzmann and K.G. Rouwenhorst, editors (2005), *The Origin of Value: The Financial Innovations that Created Modern Capital Markets*, Oxford University Press, New York.

E. Halley (1693), "An Estimate of the Degrees of the Mortality of Mankind, Drawn from the Curious Tables of the Births and Funerals at the City of Breslaw: With an Attempt to Ascertain the Price of Annuities Upon Lives," *Philosophical Transactions*, Vol. 17, pp. 596–610. (From *www.jstor.org*, Accessed 22 July 2011.)

E. Halley (1693), "Some Further Considerations on the Breslaw Bills of Mortality. By the Same Hand," *Philosophical Transactions*, Vol. 17, pp. 654–656.

G. Heywood (1994), "Edmond Halley: Actuary," *Quarterly Journal of the Royal Astronomical Society*, Vol. 35, pp. 151–154.

R.M. Jennings and A.P. Trout (1982), *The Tontine: From the Reign of Louis XIV to the French Revolutionary Era*, Huebner Foundation Monograph No. 12, Philadelphia, University of Pennsylvania.

I. Newton (1687), *Philosophiae Naturalis Principia Mathematica*, Royal Society, London.

J. Poterba (2005), "Annuities in Early and Modern Europe," Chapter 12 in *The Origin of Value: The Financial Innovations that Created Modern Capital Markets*, Oxford University Press.

H. Sherwin (1706), *Mathematical Tables*, "Chapter 7 by E. Halley on Compound Interest and Annuities," Tower Hill, London. (Accessed via Digitized by Google.)

Chapter 4: Irving Fisher

R.L. Allen (1993), *Irving Fisher: A Biography*, Blackwell Publishers, Cambridge, Massachusetts.

W.P. Bengen (2006), *Conserving Client Portfolios During Retirement*, Financial Planning Association, Denver, Colorado.

REFERENCES AND SOURCES

R.W. Dimand and J. Geonakoplos (2005), *Celebrating Irving Fisher: The Legacy of a Great Economist*, Blackwell Publishers and the American Journal of Economics and Sociology.

S. Fischer (1973), "A Life Cycle Model of Life Insurance Purchases," *International Economic Review*, Vol. 14(1), pp. 132–152.

I. Fisher and E. L. Fisk (1915), *How to Live: Rules for Healthful Living Based on Modern Science*, Funk and Wagnalls Company, New York.

I. Fisher (1930), *The Theory of Interest: As Determined by Impatience to Spend Income and Opportunity to Invest it*, The Macmillan Company, New York.

I.N. Fisher (1956), *My Father, Irving Fisher*, Comet Press, New York.

M. Friedman (1957), *A Theory of the Consumption Function*, Princeton University Press.

L.J. Kotlikoff and S. Burns (2008), *Spend 'til the End: The Revolutionary Guide to Raising Your Living Standard Today and When You Retire*, Simon and Schuster, New York.

G. Loewenstein and D. Prelec (1991), "Negative Time Preference," *American Economic Review*, Vol. 81, No. 2, pp. 347–352.

F. Modigliani (1986), "Life cycle, individual thrift and the wealth of nations," *American Economic Review*, Vol. 76(3), pp. 297–313.

R.H. Thaler (1997), "Irving Fisher: Modern Behavioral Economist," *American Economic Review*, Vol. 87, No. 2, pp. 439–441.

M.E. Yaari (1965), "Uncertain Lifetime, Life Insurance and the Theory of the Consumer," *The Review of Economic Studies*, Vol. 32(2), pp. 137–150.

M.J. Zwecher (2010), *Retirement Portfolios: Theory, Construction and Management*, John Wiley and Sons, Hoboken, New Jersey.

Chapter 5: Paul Samuelson

G.S. Becker (1993), *Human Capital: A Theoretical and Empirical Analysis with Special Reference to Education* (3rd Edition), University of Chicago Press.

P.L. Bernstein (1992), *Capital Ideas: The Improbable Origins of Modern Wall Street*, The Free Press, New York.

Z. Bodie, R.C. Merton and W. Samuelson (1992), "Labor Supply Flexibility and Portfolio Choice in a Life Cycle Model," *Journal of Economic Dynamics and Control*, Vol. 16, pp. 427–449.

Z. Bodie and M.J. Clowes (2003), *Worry-Free Investing: A Safe Approach to Achieving Your Lifetime Financial Goals*, FT Prentice Hall, Upper Saddle River, New Jersey.

W. Breit and R.W. Spencer, editors (1997), *Lives of the Laureates: Thirteen Nobel Economists*, Massachusetts Institute of Technology Press.

J.Y. Campbell and L. Viceira (2002), *Strategic Asset Allocation: Portfolio Choice for Long Term Investors*, Oxford University Press, Malden, MA.

R.G. Ibbotson Associates (2010), *Stocks, Bonds, Bills and Inflation (SBBI) Classic Yearbook*, Morningstar, Chicago.

J.M. Keynes (1936), *The General Theory of Employment, Interest and Money, Macmillan*, London.

B.G. Malkiel (2004), *A Random Walk Down Wall Street* (8th Edition), W.W. Norton and Company, New York.

H. Markowitz (1959), *Portfolio Selection: Efficient Diversification of Investments*, John Wiley and Sons.

P.A. Samuelson (1969), "Lifetime Portfolio Selection by Dynamic Stochastic Programming," *The Review of Economics and Statistics*, Vol. 51, No. 3, pp. 239–246.

P.A. Samuelson (1997), private communication with author, 18 March 1997.

P.A. Samuelson and W. Nordhaus (2004), *Economics* (18th Edition), McGraw-Hill/Irwin.

W.F. Sharpe (1964), "Capital Asset Prices: A Theory of Market Equilibrium Under Conditions of Risk," *The Journal of Finance*, Vol. XIX, No. 3, pp. 425–442.

J.J. Siegel (2002), *Stocks for the Long Run* (3rd Edition), McGraw-Hill, New York.

M. Szenberg, A.A. Gottesman and L. Ramrattan (2005), *Paul Samuelson on Being an Economist*, Jorge Pinto Books, New York.

M.W. Weinstein (2009), "Paul A. Samuelson, Economist, Dies at 94," *New York Times*, 14 December 2009.

Chapter 6: Solomon Huebner

J.B. Aponte and H.S. Denenberg (1968), "A New Concept of the Economics of Life Value: A Rationale for Term Insurance as the Cornerstone of Insurance Marketing," *The Journal of Risk and Insurance*, Vol. 35, No. 3, pp. 337 356.

G. Clark (1999), *Betting on Lives: The Culture of Life Insurance in England during the period 1695 to 1775*, Manchester University Press.

L.I. Dublin and A.J. Lotka (1946), *The Money Value of a Man* (revised edition), The Ronald Press Company, New York.

S. Haberman and T.A. Sibbett, editors (1995), *The History of Actuarial Science* (10-volume set), Pickering and Chatto, London.

A.E. Hofflander (1966), "The Human Life Value: An Historical Perspective," *The Journal of Risk and Insurance*, Vol. 33, pp. 381–391.

S.S. Huebner (1904), "The Inheritance Tax in the American Commonwealths," *The Quarterly Journal of Economics*, Vol. 18, No. 4, pp. 529–550.

S.S. Huebner (1944), *The Economics of Life Insurance: Human Life Values, Their Financial Organization, Management and Liquidation* (2nd Edition), D. Appleton-Century Company, New York.

S.S. Huebner (1922), *The Stock Market*, D. Appleton and Company, New York.

R.G. Ibbotson, M.A. Milevsky, P. Chen and K.X. Zhu (2007), *Lifetime Financial Advice: Human Capital, Asset Allocation and Insurance*, Research Foundation of the CFA Institute, Charlottesville, Virginia.

H.J. Loman (1964), "Obituary of Solomon S. Huebner," Reprinted from Annals of the C.P.C.U., pp. 320–322.

D.C. North (1954), "Life Insurance and Investment Banking at the Time of the Armstrong Investigation of 1905–1906," *Journal of Economic History*, Vol. 14, No. 3, pp. 209–228.

R.L. Ransom and R. Sutch (1987), "Tontine Insurance and the Armstrong Investigation: A Case of Stifled Innovation, 1868–1905," *Journal of Economic History*, Vol. 47, No. 2, pp. 379–390.

M.F. Stone (1960), *The Teacher Who Changed an Industry: A Biography of Solomon S. Huebner of the University of Pennsylvania*, Richard D. Irwin, Homewood, Illinois.

American Council of Life Insurers (ACLI). *ACLI Life Insurers Fact Book 2011*. ACLI, 18 November 2011, Washington.

Chapter 7: Andrei Nikolaevich Kolmogorov

S. Asmussen (2000), *Ruin Probabilities*, World Scientific Publishing, Singapore.

N.H. Bingham (2003), "A.N. Kolmogorov: 1903–1987," *EMS September*, pp. 12–13.

D. Bodanis (2000), *E=MC2: A Biography of the World's Most Famous Equation*, Anchor Canada, Toronto.

R.P. Crease (2009), *The Great Equations: The Hunt for Cosmic Beauty in Numbers*, Constable & Robinson, Ltd., United Kingdom.

J. Gleick (1987), "A.N. Kolmogorov Dies at 84: Top Russian Mathematician," *New York Times*, 23 October 1987.

M. Guillen (1995), *Five Equations that Changed the World: The Power and Poetry of Mathematics*, Hyperion, New York.

D.G. Kendall (1991), "Andrei Nikloaevich Kolmogorov: 25 April 1903 to 20 October 1987," *Biographical Memoirs of Fellows of the Royal Society*, Vol. 37, pp. 300–319.

A.N. Kolmogorov (1933), *Grundbegriffe der Wahrscheinlichkeitsrechnung*, Springer, Berlin, 1933. Translated by N. Morrison (1950) as *Foundations of the Theory of Probability*, Chelsea Publishing, Oxford, England.

A.N. Kolmogorov (1984), "An Analysis of the Metric Structure of A.S. Pushkin's Poem *Arion*," *Problems in the Theory of Poetry*, Leningrad, pp. 118–120.

E. Maor (1994), *e: The Story of a Number*, Princeton University Press.

H.H. McFaden (2000), *Kolmogorov in Perspective* (translated from Russian), American Mathematical Society, Providence, Rhode Island.

M.A. Milevsky (2006), *The Calculus of Retirement Income*, Cambridge University Press.

B. Oksendal (1998), *Stochastic Differential Equations: An Introduction with Applications* (5th Edition), Springer-Verlag, Berlin.

L. Salem, F. Testard and C. Salem (1992), *The Most Beautiful Mathematical Formulas* (translated by J.D. West), John Wiley and Sons, Toronto.

A.N. Shiryaev, A.L. Rukhin and P. Shaman (1991), "Everything About Kolmogorov Was Unusual," *Statistical Science*, Vol. 6, No. 3, pp. 313–318.

Conclusion

M.A. Milevsky (2012), "A Proper Derivation of the 7 Most Important Equations for your Retirement," working paper, available at www.MosheMilevsky.com.

ACKNOWLEDGMENTS

I can trace the origin of this project to a Saturday afternoon in mid-July 2011. I was reviewing some old academic articles and came across the 1965 classic by Menahem Yaari, in which he extended Irving Fisher's model of lifecycle consumption to include lifetime uncertainty. (Equation #4 in this book.) It is a simple, modest and beautiful expression, and I was struck by how relevant that equation still is—45 years later—for retirement income planning in the 21st century. The July weather was pleasant, the day was long, and I proceeded to muse about other noteworthy calculations and equations that are indispensable for retirement income planning. I wondered about the number of such equations, the people who deserve credit for those equations, and when they had actually been discovered. Isn't that what Saturday afternoons are all about? At some point I said to myself: "Hey, perhaps there is a book project here . . ." And so, after much digging, many conversations with advisors, friends and colleagues, six months later I completed a manuscript.

As I mentioned in the Introduction, this book is really about retirement conversations, and this project would have not been possible without the many conversations I have had over many years. In particular, I am grateful to Narat Charupat, Peng Chen, Francois Gadenne, Huaxiong Huang, Mark Kamstra, David Promislow, Chris Robinson, Tom Salisbury and Jenny Young for many enlightening conversations on these topics. I would also like to acknowledge Zvi Bodie, Larry Kotlikoff and Olivia Mitchell, three scholars whose work I greatly admire and whose writing is required reading in the growing field of retirement income planning.

As far as the book is concerned, I received excellent research, data and administrative assistance from Alexa Brand, Simon Dabrowski, Maxwell Serebryanny and Minjie Zhang. Likewise, I owe many thanks to Karen Milner, my executive editor at Wiley, as well as production editor Elizabeth McCurdy and substantive editor Andrew Tzembelicos.

It is customary for an author to end his acknowledgments by emphatically thanking his wife for providing both real and imaginary benefits that were indispensable. In the case of this particular project, I truly owe Edna (my wife) an incalculable editorial debt. She was critically involved in the design and structure of each chapter, and patiently provided feedback on every one of the drafts.

This is my 10th published book, which I strangely found the easiest to write but the hardest to finish. I continue to be fascinated by the lives and achievements of the seven scholars profiled, and could have effortlessly generated twice the number of words to describe their contributions. Of course, my editor would have accepted none of that.

ABOUT THE AUTHOR

Moshe A. Milevsky, Ph.D., is a tenured professor at the Schulich School of Business and a member of the Graduate Department of Mathematics and Statistics at York University in Toronto (Canada). He is the Executive Director of the IFID Centre and a Fellow of the Fields Institute for Research in Mathematical Sciences.

Dr. Milevsky has published 10 books, over 60 peer-reviewed research papers, and more than 200 popular magazine and newspaper articles. He has earned two National Magazine Awards (Canada), a Graham and Dodd Scroll Award (from the CFA Institute) and a lifetime achievement award from the Retirement Income Industry Association. He has given lectures and seminars all over the world and was recently selected as an MDRT (Million Dollar Round Table) Main Platform speaker.

Moshe grew up in Baltimore, New York, Mexico City and Jerusalem, and currently lives in Toronto with his wife and four daughters. You can follow him on Twitter at: http://twitter.com/RetirementQuant.

SHORT POEM

Seven equations are found in this book,
Open its pages and come take a look.
Fibonacci, Halley and many more,
Will help you live retirement with money galore.

Getting interest from the bank is a smart thing to do,
Leonardo Fibonacci will teach this to you.
Just by not spending your money can grow,
But you better pray interest rates don't go too low.

The time you will live would be nice to know,
How to predict this Benjamin Gompertz could show.
With knowledge like this you can feel free to spend,
Without any financial regrets until the very end.

Not only did Halley predict when his famous comet would come,
He also valued pensions which you get a lifetime of money from.
A true pension will bring you guaranteed money no sorrow,
But don't spend too much or from the kids you must borrow.

SHORT POEM

Irving Fisher told everyone it was unhealthy to smoke,
Sadly, he gambled all his money and then died broke.
He didn't drink coffee, tea or eat unhealthy food,
All of that probably put him in a very bad mood.

About three of these geniuses I didn't tell,
So to know the rest you must listen well.
I promise that if all the seven stories you closely follow,
After reading this book your head won't be hollow.

Maya A.T. Milevsky
Age 11, Winter 2012

INDEX

INDEX

Bengen, William, 81–82
Bernstein, Peter, 177
Bismarck, Otto von, 6
Black, Fischer, 177
Black Thursday, 99
Bodie, Zvi, 107, 116, 119
bond market, 65–66
Breslau, Poland, 55, 69
bubble tendencies, 98
buy-term-and-invest-the-difference
   (BTID) philosophy, 143–144

C
cafeteria Keynesian, 122
calculus, 159
capital asset pricing model (CAPM)
   equation, 177
Capital Ideas: The Improbable Origins
   of Modern Wall Street
   (Bernstein), 177
capital market, 85
causes of death, 49
centenarians, 48, 49–50
   see also Gompertz law of mortality
Charles II, King of England, 55–56
Chartered Life Underwriter
   (CLU), 132
Chicago school, 121–122
classical economics, 86
Clemens, Samuel, 76
Clinton, Bill, 123
common logarithms, 11, 180
compound interest calculations, 20
compounding, 20–21, 182–183
conclusion, 175–178
consumption rate, 84–85, 90*f*, 91*f*
   see also spending rate
consumption smoothing, 82, 94
continuous state-space Markov
   process, 171
continuous time Markov process, 171
Cramer, Harald, 159

credit, 175–177
credit card interest, 85–86

D
de-accumulation planning, 2
de Witt, Jan, 176
death, and probability of dying, 37
death benefit, 134, 140
   see also life insurance; life insurance
   equation
death rates, 160–161
Defined Benefit (DB) plan, 56–58
Defined Contribution (DC) plan,
   32, 57–58
demographers, 49, 54
derivatives, 160, 162
"Determining Withdrawal Rates
   Using Historical Data"
   (Bengen), 82
differential equation, 160–161,
   167–168, 170, 172
   see also Kolmogorov's equation
discount rate, 84, 85–86, 88–89
disutilities of loss, 102
divergent Fourier series, 152
diversified portfolio, 107, 149–150
Dmitrievna, Anna, 173
dollar-valued withdrawal
   rate, 155
Dow Jones Industrial Average (DJIA),
   102, 104, 105*f*, 123–124

E
e = 2.71828, 180–181, 182–183
early death of a parent, 120
economic tradeoff, 15, 50–51
The Economics of Life Insurance
   (Huebner), 129, 141
Economics (Samuelson), 120
Edgeworth, Francis Ysidro, 95
Edmonds, T.R., 176
efficient investment frontier, 177

INDEX

INDEX

knowing future rates, 24
major Italian business cities (1200-1400), 25f
nominal interest rate, 80
and pension value, 65–66
real interest rate, 21, 80, 84, 85
from safest possible investment, 112–113
subjective discount rate, 84, 85–86, 88–89, 92
Internal Revenue Service (IRS), 99
intertemporal choice, 88
irrational number, 180–181
Ito, Kiyosi, 171–172

J

Jackson, Michael, 121
James, Prince of England, 55–56
job security, 116
Johnson, Lyndon, 122

K

Kataev, Nikolai, 173
Kennedy, John F., 120, 122
Keynes, John Maynard, 78, 122
Keynesian economics, 122
Kolmogorov, Andrei Nikolaevich, 6, 24, 177
see also Kolmogorov's equation
divergent Fourier series, 152
life story, 151–153, 172–174
Monte Carlo Simulation, 153
papers, 170–171
probability theory, 170–171
transition probabilities, 171
work of, 170–171, 172
Kolmogorov School, 174
Kolmogorova, Maria, 173
Kolmogorov's equation
see also Kolmogorov, Andrei Nikolaevich
concepts, 159–162

critical assumption, 171
detailed example, 162–167
differential equation, 160–161, 167–168, 170
ruin probability mathematics, 159, 161–162, 167–170
verification that equation satisfied, 167–170
Kotlikoff, Laurence, 94

L

Laplace, Pierre-Simon, 159
law of mortality. See Gompertz law of mortality
League of Nations, 96
legacy, 5–6, 132–134, 140
Lehman Brothers, 124
Levant Company, 74
Liber Abaci (Fibonacci), 17–20, 23, 24, 26, 27, 29, 176
life annuities. See annuities
Life Extension Institute, 96
life insurance, 5–6, 51
see also Huebner, Solomon
amount of, 132
buy-term-and-invest-the-difference (BTID) philosophy, 143–144
death benefit, 134–136
human life value, 128–132
legacy, creation of, 132–134
purpose of, 128–132
term vs. whole life, 143–144
valuation of, 134–137
life insurance equation
application of equation, 139–140
different ages, examples, 137–138
the formula, 134–137
life settlements, 142–143
mortality rates, 139–140
permanent life insurance policy, 139
secondary markets, 142–143

INDEX

INDEX

crash of 1987, 103
  in long run, 104–108
  mid-to-late 1990s, 102–104
  probability of shortfall, 106–107
stocks
  see also Samuelson's equation
  expected growth rate, 112
  optimal retirement portfolio, 120
  risky stocks, 107–108
  volatility of stocks, 112, 119–120
Stocks for the Long Run (Siegel), 104
Stone, Mildred F., 127, 149
structured equity products, 120
subjective discount rate, 84, 85–86,
    88–89, 92
subjective time preference, 4
Sunny Sol. See Huebner, Solomon
survival probability. See Gompertz
    law of mortality; probability
sustainability, 6, 154–158,
    162–167, 170
  see also Kolmogorov's equation

T
Taft, William H., 97, 120
tastes, 84
The Teacher Who Changed an Industry
    (Huebner), 149
term life insurance, 143–144
Thaler, Richard, 95
*The Theory of Interest: As Determined
    by Impatience to Spend Income*

and Opportunity to Invest It
    (Fisher), 87, 95
time diversification, 107
time invariance, 107–108, 109
time on your side, question of,
    102–109
Tooke, Mary, 74
Tosca, Floria, 95
transition probabilities, 171
Truman, Harry S., 157
Twain, Mark, 76

U
utility value, 86

V
"Value of Life Annuities in Proportion
    to Redeemable Annuities" (de
    Witt), 176
volatility, 112, 119–120, 161

W
Walras, Leon, 95
Wharton School, 144, 149
whole life insurance, 143–144
withdrawal rate, 9–17

Y
Yaari, Menahem, 87, 146